STANLEY GRANT WWII

MOBILE MILITARY RADAR

By JAMES K GRANT

Copyright © 2023
James K. Grant

James K. Grant: grant.jamesk@gmail.com

All Rights Reserved

Hardcover ISBN: 979-8-9876768-2-0

E book ISBN: 979-8-9908539-4-2

Paperback ISBN: 979-8-9908539-5-9

LCCN: 2023940276

No part of this book may be reproduced or transmitted in any form or by any means, electronic, mechanical, photocopying, recording, or otherwise, without prior written permission of the publisher.

*Printed in the United States of America
on acid-free paper
by No Waste Publishing
An imprint of Accent Group Solutions
Saint Louis, MO 63126
2023*

PREFACE

As a boy I heard about my father's World War II (WWII) service at Kitty Hawk, North Carolina, North Africa, Corsica, and Italy, and saw his memorabilia and photograph album. When I moved to the Washington D.C. area, I thought about traveling to Kitty Hawk where he was stationed prior to going overseas, but without information about his time at Kitty Hawk I knew that I would not be able to relate to his service there considering that Kitty Hawk had changed dramatically since WWII. So, I never made the trip.

During a visit with Marty Grant, my brother, I mentioned that it was unfortunate that our father's WWII photographs and memorabilia were gone.

He said he had the photographs and memorabilia in containers that my father had left behind. These containers held most of the memorabilia that I had seen many years ago. More importantly, they contained the photographs and a copy of his discharge paper.

Armed with my father's WWII photographs, WWII stories, and discharge paper, I began a two-year quest to learn as much as possible about his WWII experience. My goals were to determine the location of the Kitty Hawk radar base, to develop a timeline of where he was during his service, and to put a context around his photographs.

In gathering detailed information, I made numerous visits to and spent many hours researching records at the National Archives at College Park, Maryland, and near St. Louis, Missouri, including a visit to the National Archives near Atlanta, Georgia. I also obtained many records from the Air Force History Museum at Maxwell Air Force Base, Montgomery, Alabama.

FOREWORD

This book is a history of Stanley J. Grant's WWII experience based on photos from his WWII photo album, and many other historical documents.

This history discusses his life before the war, the time he spent at Camp Grant, Rockford, Illinois; Fort Story, Virginia; Kitty Hawk, North Carolina with the 569th and 609th Signal Aircraft Warning Companies, and overseas in North Africa, Sardinia, Corsica, and Italy primarily with the 594th Signal Aircraft Warning Battalion, and with the 57th Fighter Group, 65th Fighter Squadron.

CONTENTS

INTRODUCTION P. 6

JAPANESE ATTACK PEARL HARBOR P. 8

ASSIGNMENT TO THE AIRCRAFT WARNING SERVICE AT FORT DIX NJ P. 12

THE EAST COAST AIRCRAFT WARNING SYSTEM P. 15

ASSIGNMENT TO THE KITTY HAWK DETACHMENT P. 17

KEYSTONE RADIO SCHOOL P. 33

STANLEY GRANT AND HELEN MICHALAK WEDDING P. 38

RETURN TO KITTY HAWK P. 41

ASSIGNMENT TO THE 594th SAW BATTALION FOR OVERSESAS DUTY P. 49

ARRIVAL IN NORTH AFRICA P. 52

SARDINIA AND CORSICA P. 54

THE 325th FIGHTER CONTROL SQAUDRON GOES TO FRANCE P. 61

THE PLATOONS GO TO ITALY AND WAIT FOR THE 594th P. 62

BLUE FIGHTER CONTROL SECTOR P. 63

ASSIGNMENT TO THE 57th FIGHTER GROUP, 65th FIGHTER SQUADRON P. 71

THE 65th FIGHTER SQUADRON MOVES TO NAPLES P. 72

WAITING TO LEAVE FOR THE PACIFIC THEATRE P. 73

LEAVING NAPLES AND ENROUTE TO THE PACIFIC P. 74

BOSTON HARBOR, CAMP MYLES STANDISH, AND DISCHARGE P. 86

AFTER THE WAR P. 94

STANLEY GRANT MILITARY RECORD P. 95

STANLEY GRANT WWII TIMELINE AND LOCATION 1941-1945 P. 101

ADDITIONAL PHOTOGRAPHS P. 104

HISTORY OF THE WW II EAST COAST AIR DEFENSE NETWORK P. 143

BIBLIOGRAPHY P. 154

INTRODUCTION

Stanley Grant was born into a Polish immigrant family living on the south side of Chicago, Illinois, at 8642 Colfax Avenue.

"They had bought the house in 1919. The day I was born. In ten years, they were frugal, and they knew how to do it. They paid the house off in ten years. The only thing they had to worry about was to pay the taxes. That was a big deal to scrape up the money some way and make payment." [1, 2]

His mother passed away when he was eleven. His father had limited work at the steel mills during the Depression, so everyone in the family had to contribute to the family's support.

Stanley had paper routes, a food route, and was a bus boy at a restaurant.

"If the patrons at the restaurant gave us a hard time, we would fill their water glasses up to the top so they couldn't pick them up without spilling the water." [3]

"We lived in South Chicago. That is 8642 Colfax Avenue. There were seven children and a mother and father. Father's name was Stanley Gronkiewicz, and mother's name was Maryann Stepankowska. My father was a blacksmith. We had three sisters and four brothers. Well, we start with Harriet, Edward, Clement, Casmir, Stanley, Genevieve, and Isabelle. We bought food at the corner grocery store, a combination of groceries and meat market. "[4]

"I had a food route in the summer, and I had a paper route year around. There was always something. If you were a hustler, you made a nickel or dime. I never got any expense money from my father and mother since I was eleven years old. Nothing! They didn't have anything to give me." [5]

---

[1] All text in italics are quotes of Stanley J. Grant
[2] Stanley Grant, Recorded interview for grade school project by Stanley Grant's granddaughter, Jennifer Grant
[3] Story told by Stanley Grant
[4] Edward Gronkiewicz, Recorded interviews for grade school projects by Stanley Grant's granddaughter, Jennifer Grant
[5] Stanley Grant, Recorded interviews for grade school projects by Stanley Grant's granddaughter, Jennifer Grant

"Well, I was eleven years old at the start of the Depression. All the time I was in grammar school I delivered papers one way or another, seven days or six days a week. It all depended on the route. And the lowest route I ever had was ... the newspaper was two cents a day and twenty cents a week. And, I had twenty customers, and I made a nickel a customer a week. I was making one dollar a week for delivering papers after school. My job changed a year before I was going to high school. I got a morning newspaper route for two hundred eleven papers. I delivered every morning and for that I was getting ten dollars per month. In the summertime, cut lawns. We used to get fresh fruit and vegetables from farmers. They used to come in different corners of South Chicago. They, the farmers, would come with their wagons and we'd come out with wagons and bushel baskets and buy stuff off them. We walked door-to-door knocking on [doors] asking the people if they were interested in this. To give you an idea, sweet corn, we would buy the sweet corn for five cents per dozen from the farmer and sell it for ten cents per dozen. We made a nickel a dozen. And, if we were lucky in selling our vegetables during the day, we came home with a dollar and thirty cents profit. It was a big day!" [6] "And whatever you had left it went into the stew pot for supper." [7]

"It taught us, the Depression taught us to be conservative, to be honest"[8]

"And, not to waste food. Food was never wasted in our family. To save our money so we would have money to pay our taxes and enough money to feed the family. That was the primary most important thing was feeding and clothing the family. That's what we had to do. That was the most important." [9]

"It started to change and come back slowly."

"We had more money to do things with, and that was the main thing. We had our churches and schools, we supported each other, helped other members of the family

---

[6] Stanley Grant, Recorded interviews for grade school projects by Stanley Grant's granddaughter, Jennifer Grant
[7] Gronkiewicz, Recorded interviews for grade school projects by Stanley Grant's granddaughter, Jennifer Grant
[8] Gronkiewicz, Recorded interviews for grade school projects by Stanley Grant's granddaughter, Jennifer Grant
[9] Stanley Grant, Recorded interviews for grade school projects by Stanley Grant's granddaughter, Jennifer Grant

like uncles, cousins. In return, they helped us. One thing it taught us to be conservative. We tried to improve our educations. So, we could get better jobs. It took a little while for things to improve. We went along with it. The one thing we never forgot was our strength to stay healthy and keep alive. That was the most important thing. Not to waste anything! Conservation that was it! Things improved in many ways. The more the situation improved, it made it really better and improved our condition to take care of ourselves. We were glad that it was over!"[10]

Stanley Grant earned his high school diploma and was working as an apprentice butcher prior to WW II.

JAPANESE ATTACK PEARL HARBOR

"Hitler by our writers was always taken seriously and thought he was a demigod way back before the [war] ever started in Europe because he was building up for it. And we knew something was going to happen. It actually started in thirty-nine.[11]

Before Pearl Harbor, the national feeling was that eventually we would enter the war in Europe against Hitler. Hitler was taking over everybody. And he was a killer of everybody. And, at the time he ran all over Europe trying to get into Great Britain but he couldn't because the Channel was there. He didn't have enough boats and large enough navy to bring troops across.

I remember Pearl Harbor. A group of boys were playing cards on a Sunday afternoon at my home. The radio announcer said that Pearl Harbor was attacked and bombed. And we knew we were going to go into the service for Uncle Sam.

We never had any discussions at all, of any kind with the Japanese. No there was a peace... that's right there was something going on, in my recollection, the Japanese had one of their officers over here to discuss some kind of a peace treaty. He was over discussing a peace treaty when they attacked us.

All Americans were upset. They were so upset, and they were surprised that the Japanese would pull off a stunt like that without giving us a warning. Just attacking!

---

[10] Gronkiewicz, Recorded interviews for grade school projects by Stanley Grant's granddaughter, Jennifer Grant
[11] Stanley Grant, Recorded interviews for grade school projects by Stanley Grant's granddaughter, Jennifer Grant

I think it was sort of a natural thing with us to hate the Japanese because they were the ones that attacked us without giving a warning. And they came around and gave us a dirty handed attack at Pearl Harbor while discussing a peace treaty with us.

Well, the spirit, from all the people was different. Seemed to change overnight. Everyone was interested in the war. What are we going to do with the Japanese? We were going to get together and knock the Japanese down [off] the pedestal where they belonged.

Everybody as soon as the Japanese bombed us were going into the Army, Air Force, Marines, or whatever, were going to get together a big armada and go on and attack the Japanese. Patriotism was very high in the country." [12]

"Right after Pearl Harbor my buddies and I went to enlist in the paratroopers, but I failed the physical. Later when I went in, the push was on to quickly build up the Army, and the physical standards had been lowered. So, I passed the physical exam with no problems". [13]

"Well, they drafted me. That was... see by drafting me and all the boys or young fellas... ages, I think, was from eighteen to thirty-five had to register for the draft. And, by draft I mean you had a number and a big lottery, and the first numbers, and the numbers getting pulled out, that's where you were assigned to come in. I didn't think about not going. We didn't because we were all physically able. As long, as you were physically able, we were drafted.

I was twenty-two. Well, I felt it was my duty to go out. All the other fellas in my gang around together in that age group felt the same way. It was our duty to go out there and protect the United States. Well, there were about eighteen in our group, and they all went to war. There were only three of them who were drafted before the war started. I was drafted in 1941. There was only one that got killed. We were a very lucky group! Eighteen, the whole gang!

We just followed our regular routine until the time anyone from the gang was drafted. They just left. There were some fellows that left a year before I did, a year and a half before I did.

---

[12] Recorded interviews for grade school projects by Stanley Grant's granddaughter, Jennifer Grant, and his Grandson, Michael Johnson
[13] Story told by Stanley Grant

I had no idea when I was coming back. None, nobody had an idea. You knew you were coming back after the war was over, but nobody knew at this time when it would be over.

Well, the way the situation was we were living at home together. We had an older sister that was living in the same house with us, and she had two kids. The two young ones so, she took care of everything at home.

I had two brothers, older brothers, Clem and John. They were married, but they worked at a steel mill. And certain jobs were considered critical to the war effort. You'd get a deferment and anybody working in the steel mill would be eliminated from going in the service. Clem and John did not go to war.

I lived in South Chicago at the time and had to report in the basement of a bank on 91st and Commercial. Throughout our section of the city, there must have been about eighty of us. They put us on, at that time the streetcars were still running, we were put on the streetcars. And drove on streetcars from South Chicago and 91st all the way to the Loop, where they were gathering everybody to take your tests, exams, and physicals.... Stayed there for a couple of days. The first Army camp was Camp Grant and that was in Illinois."[14]

Stanley Grant was inducted into the Army on January 5, 1942.[15] He spent his first two days at Camp Grant Illinois which was located northwest of Chicago just south of Rockford, Illinois, at the present site of the Chicago Rockford International Airport.

---

[14] Recorded interviews for grade school projects by Stanley Grant's granddaughter, Jennifer Grant, and his Grandson, Michael Johnson
[15] Enlisted Record and Report of Separation and Honorable Discharge, Stanley J. Grant, 10 October 1945

CAMP GRANT RECEPTION CENTER

CAMP GRANT

ASSIGNMENT TO THE AIRCRAFT WARNING SERVICE AT FORT DIX NJ

"From Camp Grant I was sent to Fort Dix, New Jersey. When we arrived, we were told that we were not expected and there was no room. Even though it was January and cold, we were placed in tents meant for summer camp."[16]

Fort Dix is located forty-two miles northeast of Philadelphia, Pennsylvania.

FORT DIX

---

[16] Story told by Stanley Grant

FORT DIX JANUARY 1942[17]

Fort Dix was crowded and disorganized. The four Signal Corps units at Fort Dix in January 1942 had recently been activated on December 15, 1941, and were reorganized as training units on January 17, 1942, to better manage and train recruits for the Aircraft Warning Service (AWS). The units were the 501st and 502nd Signal Aircraft Warning Regiments, the 551st Signal Aircraft Warning Battalion, and the 601st Signal Aircraft Warning Plotting Company.[18] [19] Approximately three thousand men from other army services, who for the most part had just finished basic training, were sent to Fort Dix in late December 1941 to be trained for the AWS. They came from Fort Bragg, NC, Fort Riley, KS, and Fort Croft, SC. Along with unassigned men at Fort Dix, NJ,[20] these recruits received approximately two weeks of basic training, and two weeks of specialty training prior to assignment to a tactical unit where advanced on-the-job training took place.[21] [22]

---

[17] West Jersey History Project, Images, Historic Images of Bergen County, Camp/Fort Dix, www.westjerseyhistory.org
[18] Unit History of the 501st Regiment for Period December 1941 to December 1943
[19] 551st Signal Aircraft Warning Battalion, Historical Report 1, October 1943 to December 1943
[20] 551st Signal Aircraft Warning Battalion, Historical Report 1, October 1943 to December 1943, p. 2
[21] Unit History of the 501st Regiment for Period December 1941 to December 1943 pp. 1-2
[22] Memorandum for: AFFCC Files, Subject: Conference on Training Program for Production of AWS personnel, January 17, 1942, Air Defense Section, Headquarters Air Force Combat Command, Bolling Field, D.C., P. 2

FORT DIX JANUARY 1942 (Pvt. GRANT THIRD FROM THE LEFT STANDING)

There are no detailed records for these units concerning which unit Pvt. Grant was assigned to, or what training he may have received. He was most likely assigned to the 501st Regiment that had responsibility for training enlisted men.

THE EAST COAST AIRCRAFT WARNING SYSTEM

In March 1941, four air commands designated the First through Fourth Air Forces were established within the Eastern, Central, Southern, and Western United States, respectively. Each air force created its own interceptor command with direct control of the air defense units in its area, including aircraft warning services and anti-aircraft units."[23] The task of organizing the air defense along the Eastern Seaboard was assigned to the First Fighter Command of the First Air Force. The First Fighter Command established fighter wings at Norfolk, Philadelphia, New York, and Boston.[24] On December 8, 1941, a convoy of mobile radar units departed from Fort Dix, New Jersey, for locations along the East Coast. Two of these Units were dispatched to cover areas south of the entrance to Chesapeake Bay. One unit was at Virginia Beach, Virginia, just south of Fort Story, and the other at Kitty Hawk, North Carolina, about 80 miles south of Fort Story on the Outer Banks. Later both of these units were detachments of the 569th Sig AW Reporting Co, Frontier activated on January 15, 1942, at Fort Dix.[25]

NORFOLK, VIRGINIA AREA AND KITTY HAWK, NORTH CAROLINA

Pvt. Grant's name appears on the January 31, 1942, roster, of the 569th and he was assigned to the detachment at Fort Story. The roster states that Pvt. Grant's Military Occupation Specialty (MOS) was 177, Radio Operator. He completed some basic training and specialty training about the same time the 501st SAW Reg. was assigned the responsibility to give communications training.

---

[23] The Army Air Forces in World War II, Men and Planes, Vol. VI, Edited by W. F. Craven and J. L. Cate, University of Chicago, Illinois, 1955. P. 86

[24] For more information on the history of the east coast air defense network see the History of the WW II East Coast Air Defense Network on page 142.

[25] Unit History of the 609th Signal Aircraft Warning Company, Regional, Period September 15, 1942, to December 31, 1942, p. 1

FORT STORY 1942 (Pvt. GRANT IS STANDING ON THE FAR RIGHT)

"That was the first group I was in. We were at Fort Story then. We still didn't complete our basic training that every soldier has to have a complete basic training because we were special. We were radar in the Signal Corps. That's the only excuse they had for us. Then later on when we got to Fort Story here's a place, we had private basic training. That's the marching, how to take apart your gun in the dark and put it together in the dark. And sleep any old place. Find a hole. Dig yourself a foxhole right away."[26]

The 569th reported to the Norfolk Air Defense Wing whose headquarters where at Norfolk, Virginia. The unit's mission was to give early warning of the approach of enemy aircraft through the deployment of radar Units strategically placed along the Eastern Coastline. The company was given the secondary mission of training personnel and was required to furnish cadres for overseas duty with newly activated units.[27] The objective of training was two-fold: Training in military occupational specialties to fill positions going overseas, and training of new soldiers which

---

[26] Recorded interviews for grade school projects by Stanley Grant's granddaughter, Jennifer Grant, and his grandson, Michael Johnson
[27] Unit History of the Norfolk Fighter Wing, Part I, up to 31 December 42, P. 5-6

included basic training, and continuous refresher training to maintain the efficiency and discipline of a military organization.[28]

The two detachments were charged with the operation of radar units and the transmission of reports to the Information Center at Norfolk, and each consisted of two reporting platoons. These platoons manned a radar unit for distant seaward search and another for close-in search and tracking missions.[29] The reporting detachments used a SCR 516 radar for close in reporting, and a SCR 270 radar for distant seaward reporting.[30]

Early in 1942, attention was focused exclusively on radar search operations. However, in late 1942, as conditions became more settled, attention was directed toward the training of personnel.[31]

For a time, a platoon of infantry was stationed across Kitty Hawk Road only a few hundred yards from the Kitty Hawk radar site. Their primary mission was protection of the radar site. However, late in 1943, the infantry was withdrawn.[32]

Pvt. Grant went from duty to hospital at 10 a.m. on February 5, 1941, and he returned to duty eleven days later at 10 a.m. February 16, 1942.[33] There is no record as to why Pvt. Grant went to hospital.

ASSIGNMENT TO THE KITTY HAWK DETACHMENT

On May 8, 1942, Pvt. Grant was assigned to the detachment at Kitty Hawk, North Carolina.[34]

"And, to get to Kitty Hawk, North Carolina, we had a three-mile bridge over an open straight of water right by the ocean. To move our equipment over they brought boats over…landing barges…. put it on. Us the soldiers, we got on a truck over the rickety bridge. The equipment could not go on that. The equipment was worth more than us anytime."[35]

---

[28] Unit History of the 609th Sig Aircraft Warning Company, Regional, Period January 1, 1943, to June 30, 1944 (Date of disbandment), pp. 14-15
[29] Ibid, p. 3
[30] Ibid, p. 4
[31] Ibid, p. 5
[32] Unit History of the 609th Signal Aircraft Warning Company, Regional, Period January 1, 1943, to June 30, 1944 (Date of disbandment), p. 10
[33] Morning Report, 659th Signal Aircraft Warning Company, Frontier, February 1942
[34] Morning Report, 659th Signal Aircraft Warning Company, Frontier, May 1942
[35] Recorded interviews for grade school projects by Stanley Grant's granddaughter, Jennifer Grant, and his grandson, Michael Johnson

Kitty Hawk was identified as approved station #14 on August 13, 1940.[36]

An Air Force Headquarters memo dated April 25, 1941, recommended that land acquisition and preparation be continued for the Kitty Hawk, N.C., and other East Coast Sites.[37] Land for the Kitty Hawk Camp was acquired in June 1941.[38]

Radar units were first established at the Kitty Hawk, N.C., and Cape Henry, Virginia, (Fort Story) sites during the East Coast maneuvers held by the First Interceptor Command during October 9-16, 1941, along with a Headquarters and Information Center at Norfolk, Virginia. After the maneuvers most of the military personnel left leaving only a nucleus of Signal Corps personnel at Fort Story until the return of the radar units and additional personnel after December 7, 1941.[39]

[The] Kitty Hawk "Radar [270-C]" was located on a sandy beach immediately in back of the Nags Head, Coast Guard Station[40] …… Range is 150 miles ……"[41]

---

[36] Records Pertaining to Aircraft Warning Stations 1920-1941 from RG 111, National Archives Identifier: 6782669, Container Identifier: Box 3, HMS Entry Number(s): PI-155 52, National Archives, College Park, Maryland

[37] Memo and attachment dated April 25, 1941, Headquarters GHQ Air Force, Bolling Field, D.C., Subject: Aircraft Warning Services and Air Defense, to: The Adjutant General, Washington, D.C., National Archives, Atlanta, GA

[38] Declaration of Surplus Real Property, File No: CE 602(Radar Station #14. Kitty Hawk, N.C.) to Surplus Property Board, Washington 25, D.C.

[39] Unit History of the 609th Sig AW Company, Regional, Period September 15, 1942, to December 31, 1942, p. 1

[40] The radar was located on a sandy area back of the Kitty Hawk Coast Guard Station

[41] Unit History of the 609th Sig AW Company, Regional, Period September 15, 1942, to December 31, 1942, Appendix VI, Inspection Report, 2nd Reporting Detachment, Kitty Hawk, North Carolina, December 1, 1942, p. 9

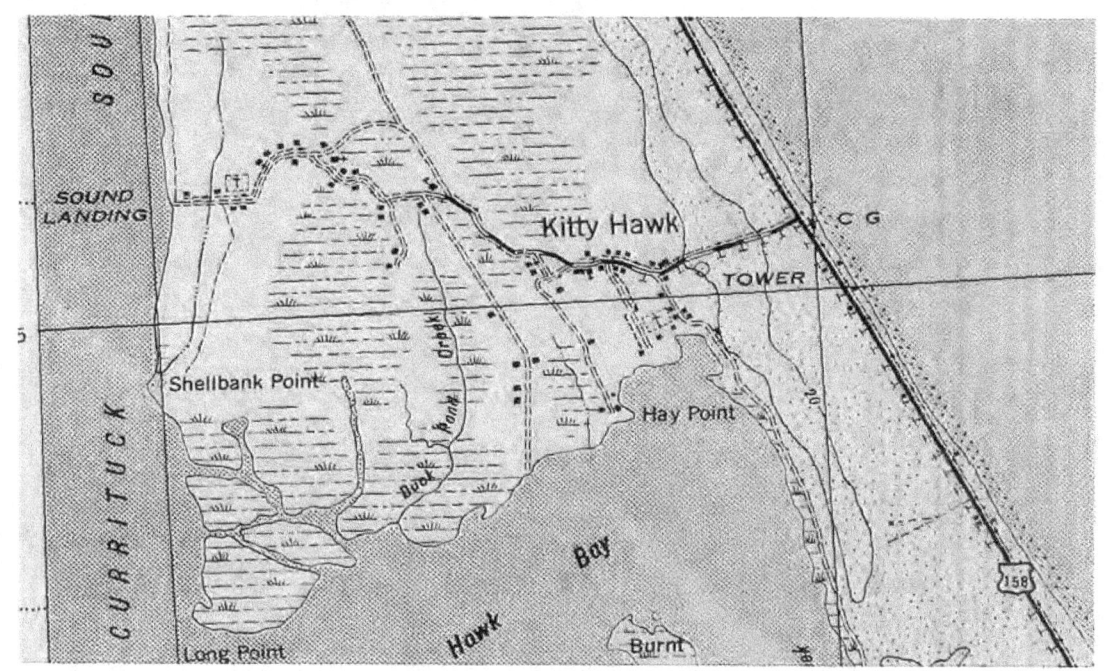

LOCATION OF THE KITTY HAWK CAMP AT THE TOWER NOTED ON THE MAP [42]

---

[42] Kitty Hawk Quadrangle, N3600-W753015, Dare County, North Carolina, 1941-1942

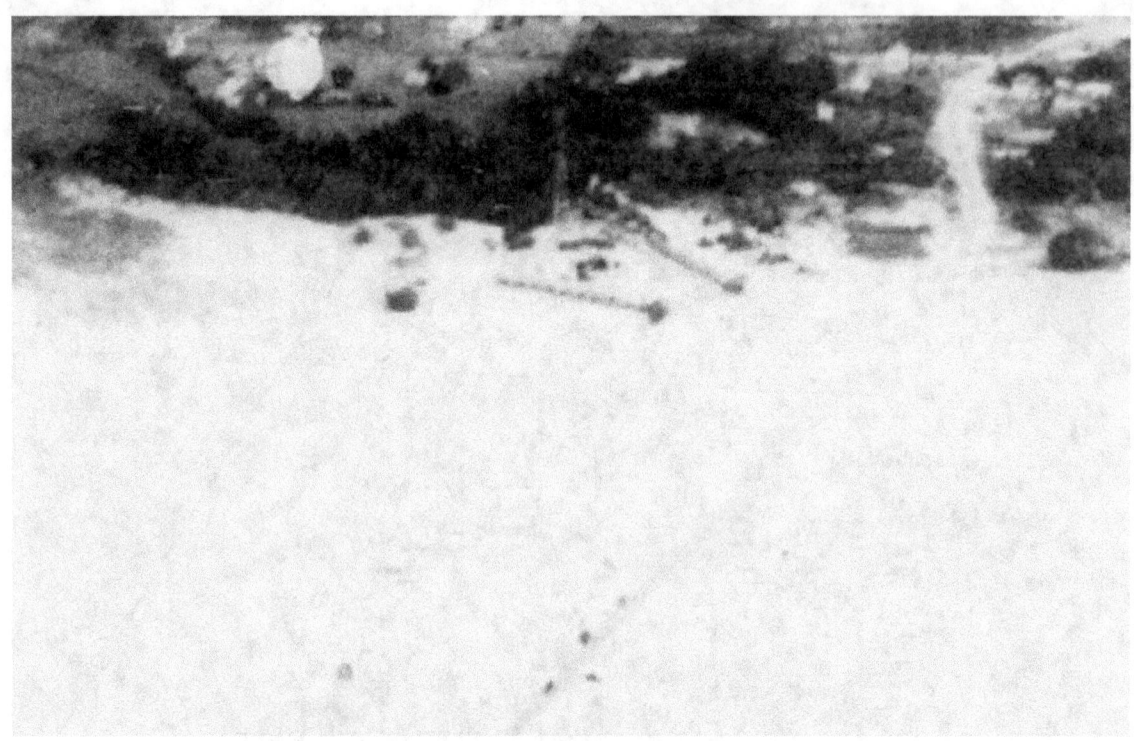

KITTY HAWK CAMP (EARLY 1942)[43]

The Kitty Hawk Camp was compact and isolated on the sand dunes. If you look closely at the camp in the above photograph you can see the faint outline of the radar tower toward the middle back of the camp just in front of the dark wooded area.

The soldiers were living and working in tents. They had to operate the radar units 24/7, but they also had other camp duties to perform as well as ongoing training. In the beginning the unit struggled with tactical and training scores. But they were learning on the fly. Ultimately, their tactical and training scores became some of the best.[44]

---

[43] Unit History of the 609th Sig AW Company, Regional, Period September 15, 1942, to December 31, 1942

[44] Unit History of the 609th Sig AW Company, Regional, Period September 15, 1942, to December 31, 1942

VIEW OF KITTY HAWK FROM TOP OF RADAR TOWER

Kitty Hawk Post Office 1943

"The main building in Kitty Hawk, at that time, was a Post Office…. in the middle of town."[45]

---

[45] Recorded interviews for grade school projects by Stanley Grant's granddaughter, Jennifer Grant, and his grandson, Michael Johnson

KITTY HAWK CAMP (X MARKS THE LOCATION OF Pvt. GRANT'S BUNK)

"Here we are our tents. That was for one platoon.... This is Kitty Hawk, North Carolina. That's when we had our new unit. Then, they were just building them. This is the way we lived. And there was nothing there but sand. And we were guarding and sweeping keeping guard, the airways open, Chesapeake Bay. They were still afraid that airplanes would sneak in."[46]

"One evening, two of us were walking back to camp. Due to the blackout along the coast, it was pitch black. A guy came along with a truck. He stopped and asked us if we wanted a ride back to camp. So, we got into the back of the truck. The lights on the truck were off due to the blackout, but he was going very fast. We got his attention and he stopped. We said how could you be going so fast when it was so dark. He said it was OK because he had the door open, and he was following the white line on the road. We decided to walk back to camp."[47]

---

[46] Recorded interviews for grade school projects by Stanley Grant's granddaughter, Jennifer Grant, and his grandson, Michael Johnson
[47] Story told by Stanley Grant

KITTY HAWK STAN 1942

"The Kitty Hawk area.... right off the beach ...was a summer resort for well-to-do people that came from Norfolk.

I'll tell you a little story. What they used to do before they came out. They got some local boys to get some all kind of game together, colored ones, and left them out on the sand dunes. Then they came back on the weekend.

So, these guys made the mistake of leaving all the colored chickens. They called them hens. We had some boys from the "Back of the Yards" in our unit from Chicago. We had plenty of ammunition… all that you wanted. There was nobody around. Birds were flying in the air in all directions! Shooting everything up! Those well-to-do people came out to do their hunting the next weekend. They wanted to know what happened to all of the game. All they could see was feathers all around. Everything was gone. GIs gone hunting!"[48]

KITTY HAWK STAN 1942

---

[48] Recorded interviews for grade school projects by Stanley Grant's granddaughter, Jennifer Grant, and his grandson, Michael Johnson

KITTY HAWK BEER STAN 1942

KITTY HAWK CHURCH ON THE BEACH 1942

KITTY HAWK STAN 1942

STAN AT KITTY HAWK BEACH 1942

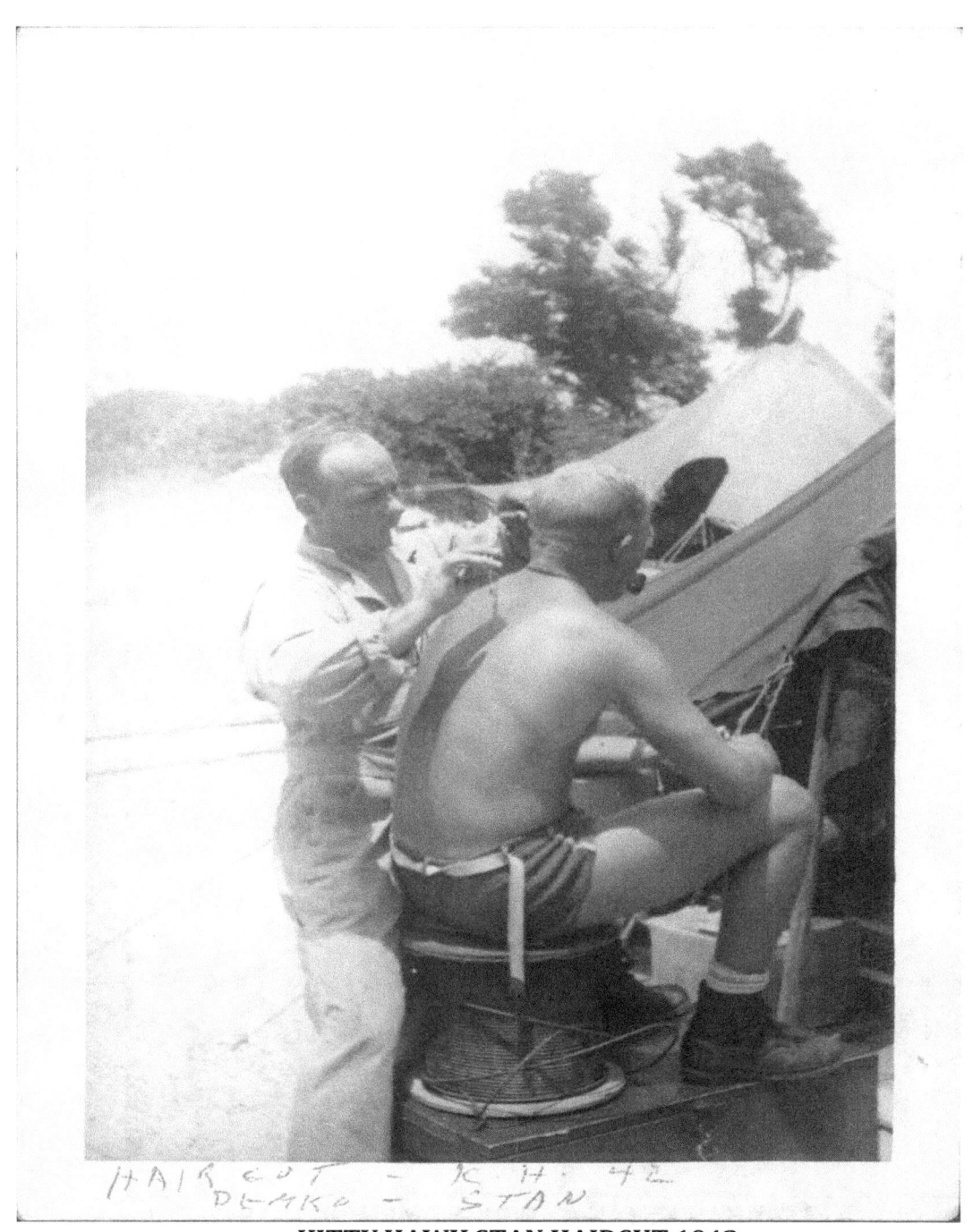
KITTY HAWK STAN HAIRCUT 1942

KITTY HAWK STAN AT WRIGHT MEMORIAL 1942

"Kitty Hawk, North Carolina, that's... where the first airplane flight was made."[49]

---

[49] Recorded interviews for grade school projects by Stanley Grant's granddaughter, Jennifer Grant, and his grandson, Michael Johnson

KITTY HAWK STAN IN FRONT OF RADAR TOWER 1942

"You don't see a picture of the radar unit. We weren't allowed to take a picture of our radar unit. Nobody was. That was a big secret then. I think the most important new technology was radar. It was picking up planes in the air from 100 to 150 miles from where you were at and sending all the information to headquarters, so headquarters knew where things were going and what was going to happen. Radar was sort of a new thing that was always handled with delicate hands."[50]

---

[50] Recorded interviews for grade school projects by Stanley Grant's granddaughter, Jennifer Grant, and his grandson, Michael Johnson

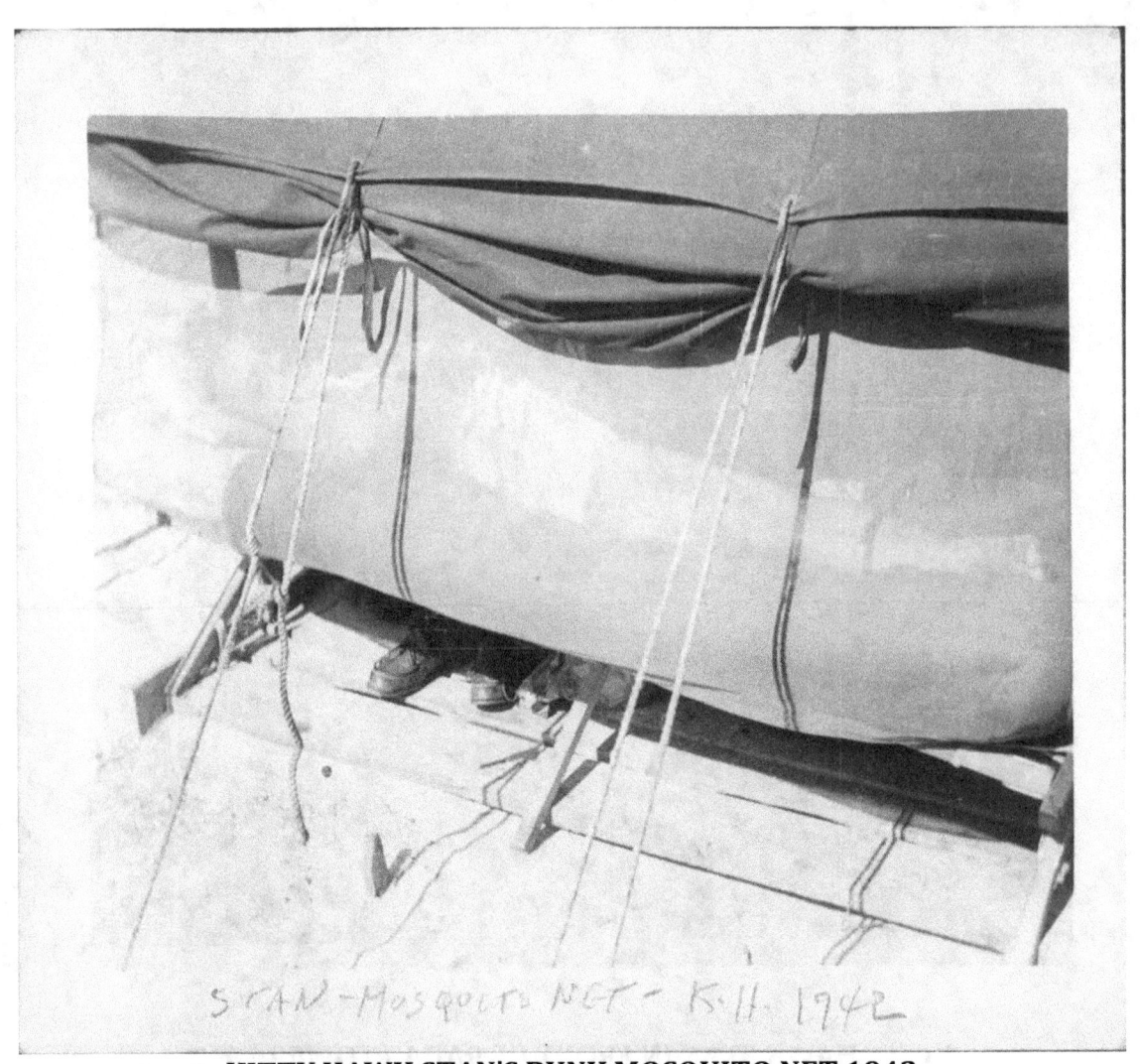
KITTY HAWK STAN'S BUNK MOSQUITO NET 1942

EDWARD KUTA-STELLA MICHALAK WEDDING MAY 1942

Pvt. Grant was on furlough from May 21 to May 27, 1942.[51] During this time, he attended the wedding of Edward Kuta and Stella Michalak on May 23, 1942, in Chicago. Stella Michalak was the sister of Helen Michalak, his future wife, also in the photograph. After the wedding he returned to duty at Fort Story.[52] Ten days later, Pvt. Grant returned to Kitty Hawk, North Carolina, on June 11, 1942.[53]

KEYSTONE RADIO SCHOOL

Pvt. Grant was assigned to the Keystone Radio School at Hollidaysburg, Pennsylvania, ninety-two miles west of Pittsburg on September 1, 1942.[54]

---

[51] Morning Report, 659th Signal Aircraft Warning Company, Frontier, May, 1942
[52] Morning Report, 659th Signal Aircraft Warning Company, Frontier, May, 1942
[53] Morning Report, 659th Signal Aircraft Warning Company, Frontier, June, 1942
[54] Morning Report, 659th Signal Aircraft Warning Company, Frontier, Sept., 1942

"In 1942, fall of 1942, I was in the service a year. Pennsylvania, I went away to radio school."[55]

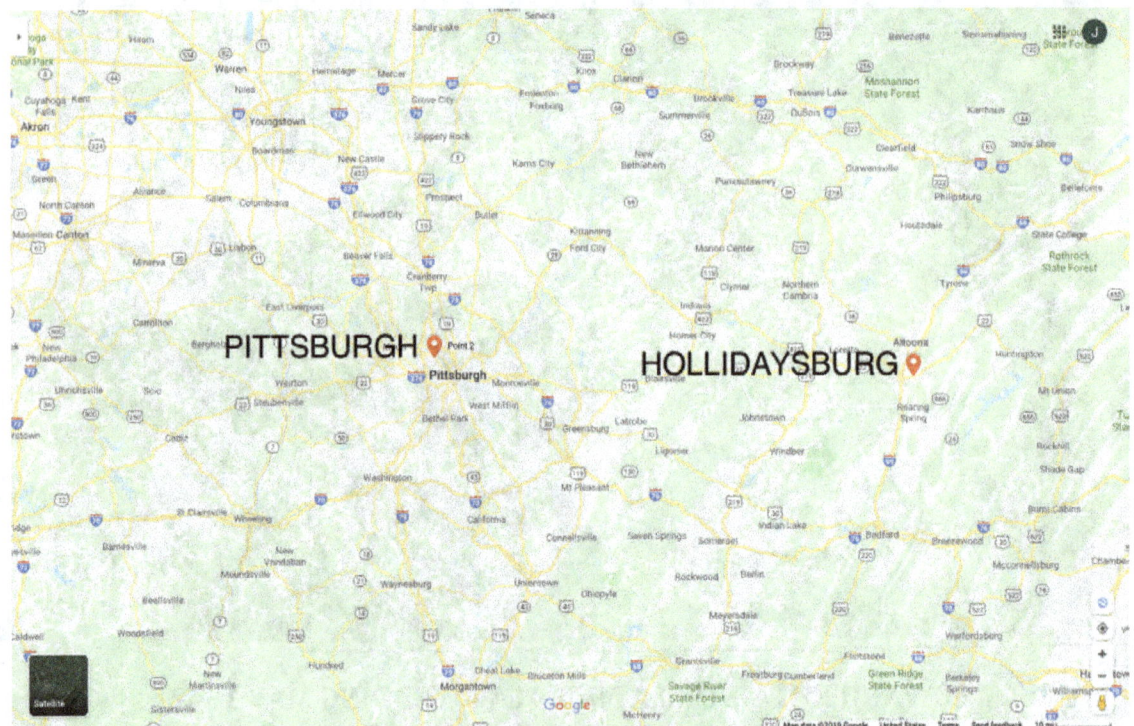

HOLLIDAYSBURG, PENNSYLVANIA

At this school Pvt. Grant learned to operate radio equipment, and to send and receive messages in Morse code.[56]

The main building at the school was Highland Hall that held the classrooms and dining facilities as well as rooms for 200-250 students. Duncan Hall, a private home, housed about 100 men. Two converted garages, also housed 90-100 men.[57]

---

[55] Recorded interviews for grade school projects by Stanley Grant's granddaughter, Jennifer Grant, and his grandson, Michael Johnson
[56] As told by Stanley Grant
[57] Annual Report of Medical Department, Keystone Radio Schools, Hollidaysburg, PA, January 4, 1943

HIGHLAND HALL MAIN BUILDING AT KEYSTONE RADIO SCHOOL

Officially this unit was the Army Signal School Detachment, Keystone Radio School Company, Third Services Command Baltimore, Maryland. The first class started on September 2, 1942.[58]

---

[58] Annual Report of Medical Department, Keystone Radio Schools, Hollidaysburg, PA, January 4, 1943

Pvt. GRANT IN FRONT OF MAIN BUILDING KEYSTONE RADIO SCHOOL 1942

Pvt. Grant was promoted to Technician Fifth Grade (T/5) on November 5, 1942, while at the Keystone Radio School.[59]

T/5 Grant was in the first class of 130 to graduate from the Hollidaysburg Keystone Radio School on the evening of November 27, 1942, after a thirteen-week intensive course for radio operators and technicians. A banquet was held in the Highland Hall

---

[59] 609th Morning Report, November 1942

School dining room followed by the commencement ceremony that was held in the Junior High auditorium. The Hollidaysburg High School Band played military music as the graduates marched into the auditorium. US Congressman James E. van Zandt expressed his hearty congratulations to the graduates. [60],[61],[62]

T/5 GRANT DIPLOMA FROM THE KEYSTONE RADIO SCHOOL

"Here is my diploma from radio school graduation. It was in Pennsylvania."[63]

---

[60] T5 Stanley Grant Keystone Radio Schools Diploma
[61] Keystone Radio Schools Graduation Ceremony Program
[62] Radio School Newspaper Article
[63] Recorded interviews for grade school projects by Stanley Grant's granddaughter, Jennifer Grant, and his grandson, Michael Johnson

T/5 STANLEY GRANT AND HELEN MICHALAK WEDDING

T/5 Grant was on furlough when he married Helen Michalak on November 21, 1942, at Chicago, Illinois.[64]

STANLEY-HELEN WEDDING NOVEMBER 21, 1942

---

[64] Stanley Grant and Helen Michalak wedding license.

MRS STANLEY GRANT NOVEMBER 1942

"Incidentally, in November 1942, Helen and I were married."[65]

Stanley Grant met Helen Michalak when he accompanied mutual friends to her house at 7133 Ingleside Avenue in South Chicago. As he passed through the kitchen,

---

[65] Recorded interviews for grade school projects by Stanley Grant's granddaughter, Jennifer Grant, and his grandson, Michael Johnson

he picked up a piece of chicken from a pot on the stove and ate it. [66] They dated from 1939 until Stanley entered the Army in January 1942. After he joined the Army, Helen wrote him a letter, but was not sure if she should send it. Her sister, Estelle, convinced her to send it. Ultimately, they were married in Chicago on November 21, 1942. [67]

MR AND MRS STANLEY GRANT NOVEMBER 1942

---

[66] Story told by Helen Grant
[67] Story as told by Helen Grant to Marilyn Grant.

RETURN TO KITTY HAWK

The 609th Morning Report, Platoon D, for December 1942 states that T/5 Grant returned to duty at the Kitty Hawk Detachment on December 1, 1942, at 6 p.m.[11]

While T/5 Grant was on duty at radio school Platoon D of the Kitty Hawk Detachment moved from tents to new barracks on November 13, 1942.[68]

Further, the 569th Reporting Company, Frontier and the 609th Signal Plotting Company, Frontier were consolidated to form the 609th Signal Aircraft Warning Company, Regional which was activated on September 15, 1942.[69]

And, by December 1942, a SCR 516 radar had been "installed about a quarter of a mile Southwest of the permanent 270-C radar.[70]

"We knew we were about to be called. The unmarried guys were going out drinking. Another married guy and I did not want to do that. So, we went on a fishing trip. When we got back all the other guys were gone. I thought I was going to be in trouble for being AWOL. But, when I reported for duty, the officer told me that he needed me to help train the new men, and that I was going to be promoted to sergeant."[71]

This fishing trip had to occur sometime between November 28th and until he reported for duty on December 1, 1942. The 609th November morning report states that two officers and twenty enlisted men (EM) were transferred to the 713 Signal Aircraft Warning Company at Drew Field, FL on November 30, 1942.[72] Earlier, 30 EM had been transferred to the 609th from the 501st Signal Aircraft Warning Regiment, a training unit, from Drew Field, FL on November 5, 1942.[73]
T/5 Grant was on furlough from December 17, 1942, to December 27, 1942.[74]
T/5 Grant was promoted to sergeant on January 1, 1943.[75]

---

[68] 609th Morning Report, Platoon D, November 1942.
[69] 609th SAW Company, Regional History 15 Sept. 1942 to Dec. 1942, P. 2
[70] 609th SAW Company, Regional History 15 Sept. 1942 to Dec. 1942, P. 9
[71] Story told by Stanley Grant
[72] Morning Report, 609th Signal Aircraft Warning Company, Regional, Nov. 1942
[73] Morning Report, 609th Signal Aircraft Warning Company, Regional, November 1942
[74] Morning Report, 609th Signal Aircraft Warning Company, Regional, Dec. 1942
[75] Morning Report, 609th Signal Aircraft Warning Company, Regional, January 1943

Sergeant (Sgt.) Grant was on furlough in Chicago from March 20, 1943, to March 27, 1943.[76]

Sgt. GRANT FURLOUGH MARCH 1943

---

[76] Morning Report, 609th Signal Aircraft Warning Company, Regional, March 1943

HELEN AND STAN IN FRONT OF MRS. BEST'S HOUSE

"Helen came to stay [for] a visit. She stayed for a couple of months."[77] She stayed with Mrs. Best at Kitty Hawk. She said that a snake had got in the house and had to be removed. She maintained correspondence with Mrs. Best during the 1950's. Stanley and Helen also visited Virginia Beach.

---

[77] Recorded interviews for grade school projects by Stanley Grant's granddaughter, Jennifer Grant, and his grandson, Michael Johnson

HELEN, MRS. BEST AND ANOTHER WIFE

HELEN AND STAN KITTY HAWK BEACH SUMMER 1943

KITTY HAWK STAN ON DUTY 1943

KITTY HAWK STAN ON DUTY 1943

KITTY HAWK INSPECTION 1943

The following are comments from an inspection report of the Second Reporting Detachment at Kitty Hawk dated July 30, 1943:

"General conditions of the installation are far from good, but it seems that much more might be done for the welfare of the EM [Enlisted Men] in many ways. The entire recreational and free time plans are left to a non-commissioned officer who attempts to do a good job but lacks vision. The officers are not assuming the responsibility delegated to them in promoting activities for the welfare of the men. Perhaps the idea that the Kitty Hawk installation is a "Little Siberia," for both the officers and EM may be responsible for the lackadaisical attitude. The non-commissioned officer with whom this officer talked was unshaven, my judgment would be that he had shaved on Sunday (two days previous). He was dressed in a fatigue uniform, apparently thrown around him hastily, and on his feet were bedroom slippers. The general appearance of the group was about the same."[78]

---

[78] 609 SAW Company, Regional Period 1 January 1943 to 30 June 1944(Date of Disbandment), Appendix 3, Report of Visit to Second Reporting Detachment, 609th Company, July 30, 1943

In the response to the inspection report:

"The entire recreation and free time plans are not left to a non-commissioned officer. The Detachment Commander always has held the responsibility. The Detachment Commander has complained bitterly about the Second Reporting Detachment being referred to as "Little Siberia," and the Company Commander, 609th has used forceful measures to stop it. True the non-commissioned officer was unshaven. The inspection was before and during breakfast and MSgt Hughes and the Detachment Commander were unable to eat breakfast until 0930. The fatigue uniform is prescribed here. True MSgt Hughes wore bedroom slippers. Two days previous MSgt Hughes walked the most part of 60 miles to be on time for duty in the morning. Capt. WOODS, M.C., advised MSgt Hughes to stay off his feet for a few days due to blisters."[79]

ASSIGNMENT TO THE 594th SAW BATTALION FOR OVERSESAS DUTY

Sgt. Grant was assigned to the 594th SAW Battalion by order of the Norfolk Fighter Wing on November 16, 1943.[80] And, he was further assigned to Company A, 2nd Platoon.[81]

The 594th was activated on November 13, 1943, at Fort Dix. The majority of the officers and enlisted personnel arrived between November 13 to 21, 1943. And the 594th was full strength on November 30, 1943. The unit consisted of a Headquarters & Plotting Company and two radar companies with a total of 913 men.[82]

Starting on December 11, 1943, Sgt. Grant was on duty at Bradley Field, Windsor Locks, Connecticut,[83] fourteen miles north of Hartford, Connecticut, and he returned to duty at Fort Dix on December 17, 1943.[84]

---

[79] Response to Report of Visit to Second Reporting Detachment, 609th Company Report of Visit to Second Reporting Detachment, 609th Company, July 30, 1943
[80] Special Order Number 5, 594th Signal Aircraft Warning Battalion, November 18, 1942, p. 1
[81] Ibid, p. 1
[82] Diary of the 594th Signal Aircraft Warning Battalion, p. 1
[83] Morning Report, 594th Signal Aircraft Warning Battalion, December 11, 1943
[84] Morning Report, 594th Signal Aircraft Warning Battalion, December 17, 1943

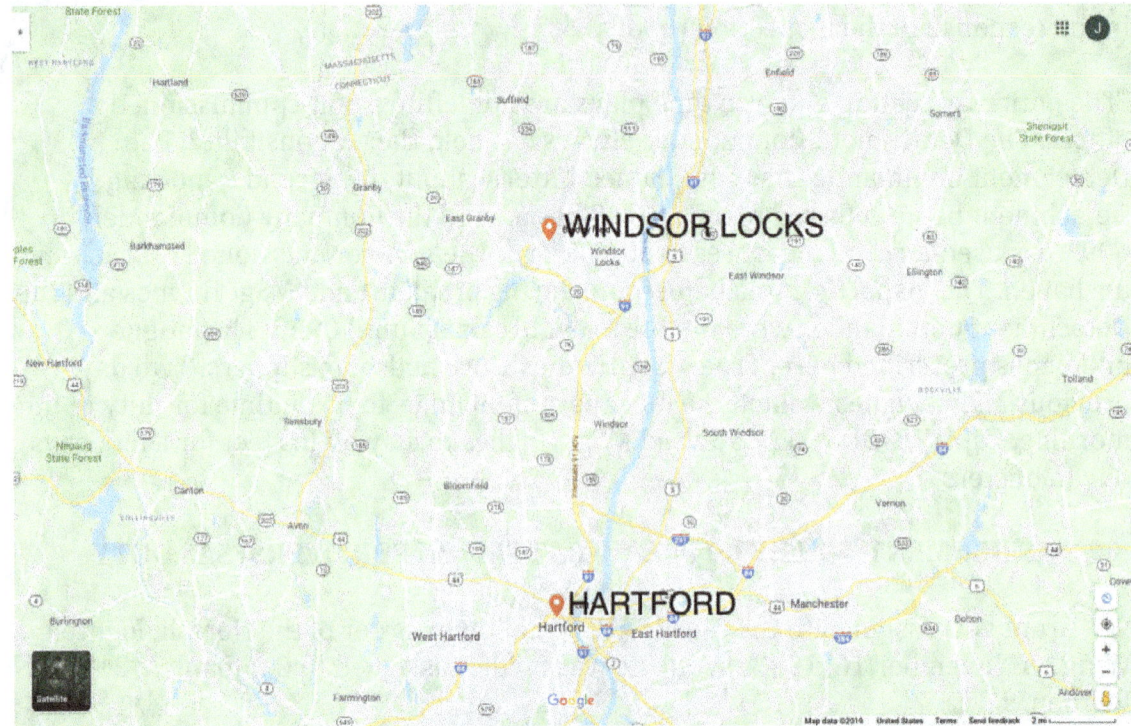

WINDSOR LOCKS

The 594th was organized and preparing to go overseas from late November 1943 through early January 1944. The Call to Port was received on December 22, 1943, and the final orders were to arrive at Camp Patrick Henry, Virginia, located twenty-nine miles north of Norfolk on January 4, 1944. The unit left Fort Dix on January 3, 1944. Travel was by rail in two sections of Pullman cars. The first section departed at 2100 hours and was followed one hour later by the second section. The 594th marched to Area No. 2 where it was stationed.[85]

"The way I got overseas we came over on a troop ship and went to North Africa. After we were overseas, we didn't have a lot of pictures. We had a camera. But we weren't supposed to take pictures."[86]

The Headquarters and Plotting Company, Company A, and Company B left Camp Patrick Henry at separate times on January 12, 1944, each boarding separate troop ships at Hampton Roads, Virginia, twenty miles north of Norfolk. The Headquarters and Plotting Company boarded the S.S. Cornelius Gilliam; Company B boarded the S.S. James Barber; and Company A boarded the Cornelius Harnett.[87]

---

[85] Diary of the 594th Signal Aircraft Warning Battalion, pp. 3-4
[86] Recorded interviews for grade school projects by Stanley Grant's granddaughter, Jennifer Grant, and his grandson, Michael Johnson
[87] Diary of the 594th Signal Aircraft Warning Battalion, pp. 4-5

USS CORNELIUS HARTNET[88]

On January 13 all three ships departed dock and anchored in the channel at Hampton Roads, VA. At 10 a.m. on January 14, 1944, all three ships departed from anchorage for an unknown destination. Heavy weather was experienced on the second day out, causing the ship to roll and resulting in more than 50 percent seasickness. The weather for the remainder of the trip was ideal.[89]

"There was a storm and I, and many others became seasick. We could not go on deck. Drums were set for the men to vomit into. But the drums filled up and were sliding around due to the rolling of the ship spilling vomit on to the floor. Some men in their bunks were vomiting down. I finally crawled into a space where life preservers were stored, and I remained there until the storm ended and I felt better. My buddies brought me some food. After the storm sailors came inside and hosed everything down."[90]

"It was good to make friends with the cooks because they would sneak out food the officers were getting such as steaks to us at night."[91]

---

[88] http://www.armed-guard.com/liberty.html
[89] Diary of the 594th Signal Aircraft Warning Battalion, pp. 4-5
[90] Story told by Stanley Grant.
[91] Story told by Stanley Grant.

*"Toward the end of our voyage we came into the Mediterranean Sea. We were all **very scared** because we could hear explosions going off which were probably due to destroyers dropping depth charges."*[92]

ARRIVAL IN NORTH AFRICA

Three ships carrying the 594th arrived on February 1, 1944, at the Harbor of Oran, Algeria. By February 3, 1944, the entire 594th was quartered in Mediterranean Base Section, Staging Area No. 2.[93]

On February 13, 1944, an advance detail departed the staging area to set up tents and to prepare for the 594th at its new location, Port of Mostaganem, Algeria. The remaining personnel of the 594th departed for Mostaganem on February 16, 1944. The movement was a 35-mile trip made by truck to set up the 594th in an area suitable for operational training.[94]

NORTH AFRICA

---

[92] Story told by Stanley Grant
[93] Diary of the 594th Signal Aircraft Warning Battalion, p. 5
[94] Ibid, pp. 5-6

The 594th was first assigned to the XII Air Support Command on 20 February 1944, and further assigned to the 64th Fighter Wing on February 23.[95] Effective March 12, 1944, the 594th was assigned to the XII Fighter Command.[96]

From March 28, 1944, to April 5, 1944, the platoons of Companies A and B departed from the 594th camp area for operational training at selected sites. The radar platoons were spread out along the North African coast. On March 28, 1944, the 1st Platoon Co A was sited at Cape Carbon, the 2nd Platoon Co A was at Ouilles, the 5th Platoon Co A was at Cape Kramis and the 6th Platoon Co B at St Cloud. On March 30, 1944, the 3rd Platoon Co A departed for Cap Kremis, and on March 31, 1944, the 2nd and 3rd Platoons Co B, departed for sites located at Dellys, Cap Figalo, and Cap Falcon, respectively[97]. Sgt. Grant was with the 2nd platoon Co A at Ouilles.[98].

"As we were driving an Arab was crouched down along the side of the rode. He was waving at us shouting "Hello Yankees!". When he got up, we saw a terd where he had been crouched down. We saw Italian prisoners of war who were laughing at us saying our war is over, but you still have to fight."[99]

"The worst memory of the war and it seems to come back now... It was an odd one. It happened in North Africa. We were in convoy and another French convoy was passing on the other side of us. And a bunch of little kids came up. There were GIs around. We had hard candy... used [to] throw them to the kids. For some reason one of the boys, he was about 10-11 years old, slipped and fell. The other kids got off the road. And this big GI truck driven by a French driver ran into the boy and knocked him down. The front wheel was up against his ribs. We thought he was going to come out. Our convoy stopped. We're gonna get the boy out. But the French driver got excited. Instead of putting in reverse, he put it in forward and ran right over the kid. And everything was splattered right in front of us. That was always getting that recollection seeing that kid get splattered up front."[100]

A 594th General Order on April 8, 1944, authorized many "deserving enlisted men" of the 594th "to wear the Good Conduct Ribbon" which included Sgt. Grant.[101]

---

[95] Ibid, p. 6
[96] Ibid, p. 7
[97] Diary of the 594th Signal Aircraft Warning Battalion, p. 9
[98] 594th Co A War Diary, June 1946
[99] Story told by Stanley Grant.
[100] Recorded interviews for grade school projects by Stanley Grant's granddaughter, Jennifer Grant, and his grandson, Michael Johnson
[101] Diary of the 594th Signal Aircraft Warning Battalion, p. 9

The following text was included with the 594's War Diary:

"In the meantime, what of the platoons? Headquarters settled down on the Mostagenum quays, where only the breaking waves dashed high over the enlisted men's latrine, and the platoons sallied forth in search of war.

From Cap Kremis west to Arzew the platoons scattered, and Algeria rested secure from attack, with only the native wine stocks in danger. HQ plotted planes and plans; the platoons reported planes and collected mascots. The First Platoon, Company A, set up at Cap Carbon, directly in line with a naval gunnery range. No casualties.

[Sgt. Grant's platoon] set up at Ouilles, near a previously placed British unit. They repelled one attack, by native dogs, and spent the rest of the time trying to barter anything at all for their neighbor's whiskey rations.

Company A's Third Platoon, together with the Fifth Platoon, were sent to Cap Kremis to report directly to the British Information Center in Oran. Aside from the gassing (tear) of an Arabian village their stay was almost without incident.

The Sixth Platoon of Co B set up at St. Cloud and reported from a field devoted to barley. The rest of Co B scattered up and down the coast of northern Africa. The most envied spot being occupied by the 4th Platoon at Perregaux, where the PX warehouse was located.

But the Dolce Far Niente of this life was rudely disturbed for the Second, and Third Platoons of Company A and the Fifth Platoon of Company B. Orders came to move. Where? Rumor was rife, and by the time the units reassembled in Mostagenum one could choose the location that best suited and proclaim its truth as vociferously as desired."[102]

SARDINIA AND CORSICA

"North Africa that was the first country that I was in. And, from North Africa I went to the islands of Sardinia and Corsica. And went from Corsica to Italy. North Africa, that's French. Sardinia, that's Italian. Corsica, that's French. Then I went back to Italy."[103]

---

[102] Draft text at end of the Diary of the 594th Aircraft Warning Battalion
[103] Recorded interviews for grade school projects by Stanley Grant's granddaughter, Jennifer Grant, and his grandson, Michael Johnson

Colonel Wagner, commanding officer of the 594th, returned in late April 1944, from a 10-day mission to the islands of Corsica and Sardinia. And 4 officers and 97 EM of the 325th Fighter Control Squadron arrived May 8, 1944, at the 594th area.[104]

On May 6, 1944, the 1st Platoon, Co A, led by Lt. Dickler departed for the Port of Oran at 0700 hours and was assigned to the 311th Fighter Control Squadron[105] to be stationed at the Island of Sardinia, Italy.[106] Two days later they landed in Sardinia.

The following is taken from the 594th' Diary:

"Here they [Company A, 1st Platoon] bought souvenirs and climbed mountains, usually arriving at one peak in time to be informed that it was on the wrong mountain. At last, running out of new mountains to climb the unit was transferred to Corsica, on September 10, with the Second and Third Platoons of more anon. But before leaving Sardinia they paused on one mountain long enough to bag two German planes, and, naturally, paint two swastikas on the side of their operational van. These symbols gave rise to one of the historic remarks of the war. A sailor aboard the ship taking the platoon to Italy looked at the van, scratched his head, and demanded of anyone within earshot: "Now, wotinell have they got in that box that can kill Germans?"[107]

"The next platoons to leave were the Second (Sgt. Grant's platoon) and Third of Company A and the Fifth of Company B. On the 24th[108] of May they went to Corsica on a French cruiser, the Emil Bretin, of which the less remembered, the better. At best a cruiser is not a pleasure boat, and in any kind of a swell the Emil Bertin was not at her best."[109] They departed from the 594th area at 0600 hours and boarded the cruiser in the Port of Oran at 1700 hours. The following day they arrived at a staging area on the Island of Corsica at Ajaccio, France, for tactical operations with the 325th Fighter Control Squadron. "[110]

---

[104] Diary of 594th Signal Aircraft Warning Battalion, p. 11 and May War Diary p. 4.
[105] 594th Co A, War Diary, May 1944
[106] 594th War Diary, May 1944, and Diary of the 594th Signal Aircraft Warning Battalion, p. 13
[107] Draft text at end of the Diary of the 594th Aircraft Warning Battalion.
[108] 594th Co A, War Diary, May 1944
[109] Ibid.
[110] 594th War Diary, May 1944, and Diary of the 594th Signal Aircraft Warning Battalion, p. 13

FRENCH CRUISER EMILE BERTIN[111]

---

[111] https://en.wikipedia.org/wiki/French_cruiser_%C3%89mile_Bertin

CORSICA

Although the 594th Battalion and Company A records say that Sgt. Grant's platoon went directly to Corsica, during interviews with his granddaughter and grandson he states that he was in Sardinia.[112] Further, the June War Diary of the 325th Fighter Control Squadron says that they completed their move from Alghero, Sardinia, to Corsica by June 13, 1944. Because his platoon was attached to the 325th, it must have joined the 325th in Sardinia before they moved to Corsica.[113]

"We went overnight on a French ship. We wanted to smoke so a French sailor took us to a place inside the ship. Later, we realized that we were smoking outside the door of an ammunition magazine. Our equipment was on a much slower freighter that had to hug the shore and follow a longer route due to the threat of submarines. So, it was a couple of weeks before our equipment arrived."[114] *Their radar was an SCR 527.*[115]

"Well, we were radar unit operators, and I was a Morse code Crew Chief to send the information back to headquarters. Everyone was busy all the time. I was trained as a Morse code operator."

---

[112] Separate recorded interviews for grade school projects by his granddaughter, Jennifer Grant, and his grandson, Michael Johnson.
[113] 325th Fighter Control Squadron War Diary, June, 1944
[114] Story told by Stanley Grant.
[115] 325th Fighter Control Squadron War Diary, July, 1944

SCR 527 RADAR IN OPERATING POSITION

The fellas, the shift on a crew, the radio operators worked hand in hand with the radar unit. They worked eight hours on and twenty-four hours off. You had four crews.

Well, your primary after we first set up the units, we were the first ones to contact headquarters.... Sent information from the radar unit sent to headquarters. And, eventually in Italy, they took over the phone lines because it was quicker and faster to get the information than in Morse code...dah.dit...dit...dah...that takes a bit longer than by voice. Then after that we were on standby in case the phone lines were down. We had to have somebody there to relay the information. Sometimes you exchanged your call letters with headquarters. There was somebody at headquarters to receive it to see if you were there ready to operate.

We were always with the radar after the combat was over. After the enemy retreated then we went into it. We weren't at the front lines. It wasn't that we were not wanting to go. Every time we moved our unit from one spot to another, we had to get engineering to come over and check for mines. Sweep it with a mine detector all over to make sure when we pulled off none of us got hurt or explosion or something. In other words, the most important thing we had, not us, it was the equipment." [116]

---

[116] Separate recorded interviews for grade school projects by his granddaughter, Jennifer Grant, and his grandson, Michael Johnson.

SCR 527 RADAR ANTENNA

"The radar platoons staged just out of town, the first of a long series of camps that were to take them all over Corsica and finally, leave two of the three units stranded, weeks later, on a garbage dump south of Bastia. But, unaware of their fate, the men cheerfully accepted the 325th F.C.S. as their new headquarters and devoted the summer to an official tour of Corsica."[117]

From June 1-13, 1944, the 325th was moving from Alghero Camp on Sardinia, Italy to a new headquarters camp at Calvi Air Base, Corsica. By June, 1944, their base of operations was set up at Calvi.[118] By June 22, the 594th Co A, 2nd (Sgt. Grant's platoon) and 3rd Platoons were at Cateraggie, Corsica near Ghisohaccia, Corsica [119] fifty-one miles south of Bastia, Corsica. While the 594th Co A 1st Platoon was still on duty in Sardinia, and the 4th and 5th Platoons were still in North Africa.[120]

---

[117] 325th Fighter Control Squadron War Diary, June, 9144
[118] Ibid., p. 1
[119] Ibid., p. 2
[120] 594th Co A, War Diary, June, 1944

"At the rate I was going, I wrote letters home once about every two weeks."[121]

"In Corsica, crossing the Mediterranean Sea the German fighter planes used to come over and strafe the airport. I was lucky. I was in my foxhole. When you get over there the first thing you do is dig a hole that's called a foxhole. That was the best place to be when somebody started shooting at you. So, I was lucky I never got hurt. Other guys got shot up a little bit. I went through the whole campaign without getting injured."[122]

"There were many times that I didn't think I was going to make it. I was off duty during the day and was sleeping in a house where we had set up camp. There was a farmyard where we spread out the radar from the radio to the farmhouse. We had placed boardwalks down between these areas. Before we moved in the engineers had swept the area for mines and as usual our officer had the area swept twice. Because it was very hot, I was sleeping in the nude. I suddenly woke up due to a loud explosion. So, I grabbed and put on my helmet, and I ran out of the building and jumped into my foxhole. Next thing I know is that fellow soldiers were standing around my foxhole looking down at me laughing. A cow had wondered into the farmyard and stepped on a mine that the engineers had not detected. Had any of us wandered off the boardwalk, we could have been killed rather than the cow."[123]

Corsica was strategically important because it served as a base for bombers and fighters supporting US and British ground forces as they fought north up the Italian peninsula. There were seventeen air bases on Corsica. Therefore, its nickname was the USS Corsica. [124] Until US ground forces advanced to Pisa and beyond in early September 1944, the US airbases on Corsica were subject to attack by German aircraft.

---

[121] Separate recorded interviews for grade school projects by his granddaughter, Jennifer Grant, and his grandson, Michael Johnson.
[122] Recorded interviews for grade school projects by Stanley Grant's granddaughter, Jennifer Grant, and his Grandson, Michael Johnson
[123] Story told by Stanley Grant.
[124] U.S.S. Corsica, L'ile Portes Avions, Dominique Taddei, Albiana, 2003.

CORSICA 1944

THE 325th FIGHTER CONTROL SQUADRON GOES TO FRANCE

"The 325th, having gathered unto itself additional plotting and communications personnel from the 594th, left for France 29 June leaving the Co A, 2nd (Sgt. Grant's platoon) and 3rd platoons bogged down in the refuse south of Bastia, arrived rejoicing in France and set up headquarters at San Tropez. Ready for any eventuality they stood poised to repel any attempt of the Luftwaffe to bomb the invasion beaches. After all, it wasn't their fault that there was no Luftwaffe."[125]

"In the meanwhile, the sole representative of B Company left Napoleon's isle, the 2nd of July and arrived at PlAMBINO, Italy, on the 5th. From there their history merged

---

[125] From draft text at end of the Diary of the 594th Aircraft Warning Battalion.

with the Italian Legend until their return to the parent organization at Coltano, Italy, in October."[126]

On September 10, 1944, 1st Platoon Co A left Sardinia to join the 2nd and 3rd Platoons on Corsica.[127] The 2nd and 3rd Platoons were released from service with the 325th as of September 10, 1944.

THE PLATOONS GO TO ITALY AND WAIT FOR THE 594th

There is no information as to exactly how or when the 1st, 2nd, and 3rd platoons from Company A got to Italy. They were still in Corsica in September 1944, and they went to Italy sometime during October most likely by LST. They were at Coltano, Italy, prior to the arrival of the 594th in late November 1944.

"Came October – which means rain in Italy, and as the rains came, so came the wandering platoons, by LST, by liberty, and by truck to the mud-be smeared remnants of Mission 16, still bogged down in the Pisa airfield.

The final gathering of the clans was marked by the flood of November and by tractor, truck, and water-wings units and men were moved to Coltano as headquarters for the rest of the war."[128]

"The equipment detail [of the 594th] arrived at Leghorn, Italy on November 4, 1944, and proceeded to ... the Bn Camp Area, (Coltano, Italy), where it joined personnel of Mission 16 and many former members of the Battalion who had departed with the X-Sector [Corsica] several months ago.[129]

---

[126] Ibid.
[127] 594th War Diary Co A, September 1944
[128] Draft text at end of the Diary of the 594th Aircraft Warning Battalion.
[129] 594th War Diary, Co A, November 1944

SARDINIA, CORSICA, AND ITALY

Meanwhile, the 594th moved from North Africa by ship via a stop at Peninsular Base Section Staging Area No. 1 at Bagnoli, near Naples. The 594th started disembarking their troop ship at Leghorn, Italy, at 1300 hours on November 21, 1944.[130] Company A disembarked "at 1600 hours and rode by truck to the Battalion Area at Coltano – a point midway between Livorno and Pisa. Company A was finally back to old company strength again on November 26, 1944. And had the good fortune of meeting some old personnel again."[131] Sgt Grant's platoon was with company A at this time.

BLUE FIGHTER CONTROL SECTOR

The 594th and the 78th Fighter Control Squadron comprised the Blue Fighter Control Sector. The two organizations were in adjacent areas[132] seven miles south of Pisa just off the highway to the west."[133]

---

[130] 594th War Diary, May 1944, and Diary of the 594th Signal Aircraft Warning Battalion, pp. 26-28.
[131] 594th War Diary, Co A, November 1944.
[132] 594th History, The War & the 594th, p. 5
[133] 78th Fighter Control Squadron, War Diary, November 1944

The following is taken from draft text at the end of the 594th Diary:

"Africa, Corsica, Sardinia, France, and Italy were all learning that the 594th had arrived, and all concerned were taking the news with remarkable calmness. But still another country was ticketed to bear the brunt of this organization's remarkable thirst for souvenirs. Mission 16, destined for Russia, was conceived in Mostagenum July 29, 1944, left for Italy August 30, and died in the mud of Pisa airfield.

There is limited information on the specific locations of the platoons in Italy.

Once again, the platoons moved out, and the winter was spent in defending everything from Livorno to the Serchio and from Marina di Pisa to Pondidera"[134]

By the end of November, Sgt. Grant was with the 2nd Platoon operating at Montanero.

On December 9, 1944, Lt. Johnson, Commanding Officer, 2nd Platoon, Co B, reported that his platoon, located at Mt. Meto Mommio Italy had been fired upon. Six shells had landed directly in the camp area. The shells were coming from the 366th Infantry Regt. 92nd Div. The 366th had established a tactical training site nearby and its members were unaware of the presence of the 2nd platoon.

The 2nd Platoon, Co A moved on March 24, 1945, from the site at Montanero, Italy, to Castelfranco, Italy.[135]

On April 12, 1945, Helen Grant was working as a telephone operator in Chicago when President Roosevelt died. She said her switchboard lit up like a Christmas tree from all the calls being placed.[136]

---

[134] Draft text at end of the Diary of the 594th Aircraft Warning Battalion.
[135] 594th War Diary, May 1944, and Diary of the 594th Signal Aircraft Warning Battalion, p. 39.
[136] Story as told by Helen Grant.

594TH PLATOONS NOVEMBER-DECEMBER 1944

"With a concerted blast of guns and publicity the allied drive into the Po [River valley] started in April. And, close upon the heels of the triumphant armies came the 594th, not in strength, true, but in echelon."[137]

"As a radio operator I could tune into the BBC and get the news on how the war was going. I could also listen in on the chatter of the fighter pilots. If a British pilot's plane was hit, he would say my kite is on fire and I am going down. On the other hand, the American pilots would curse a blue streak."[138]

[There is limited information on the locations of the platoons in the Po River Valley.]

The group, under Lt. Hamilton, moved into Bologna, out of Bologna, and finally settled in a lavishly boob-trapped villa on the outskirts of Bologna.

"The radar units came after the combat troops. The radar equipment was more important than the men. The engineers would check for mines."[139]

---

[137] Draft text at end of the Diary of the 594th Aircraft Warning Battalion.
[138] Story told by Stanley Grant.
[139] Recorded interviews for grade school projects by Stanley Grant's granddaughter, Jennifer Grant, and his Grandson, Michael Johnson

The platoons were at Bologna, Verona, Villa Franca, San Vito, Milano, San Felice, and Parma [140], Grosseti, and Pal'zo Cataldi, Italy.[141]

594TH PLATOONS APRIL- MAY 1945

"The war ended in 1945. In May, May 3, I think it was the first one then about a week later in Europe the rest of the Germans surrendered. That ended the war in Europe. But the war in the Pacific was still going on."[142]

By the end of May all the platoons were back at the battalion area at Coltano, Italy.

---

[140] Draft text at end of the Diary of the 594th Aircraft Warning Battalion.
[141] Diary of the 594th Signal Aircraft Warning Battalion, p. 40.
[142] Recorded interviews for grade school projects by Stanley Grant's granddaughter, Jennifer Grant, and his Grandson, Michael Johnson

ITALY 1945 Sgt. GRANT IS FIFTH FROM THE LEFT

Sgt. GRANT ITALY 1945

ITALY 1945 T/5 EMBICH and Sgt. GRANT ON THE RIGHT

THE MEN Sgt. GRANT WORKED WITH MOST WHILE WITH THE 594TH
Left to right: Top row: Stadler, Kraft, Macal, Embich
Bottom: row: Petrosene, Heiden

"Thus the 594th and the war. Our casualties, none. Our journies, many. Our decorations? Captain Zais, Sgt Leisering, Tec 4 Taylor wear the bronze star for their work in France. The First Platoon of Company A has been commended for their work in Sardinia. The Second (Sgt. Grant's platoon) and Third Platoons of Company A received letters from SHEAF [Supreme Headquarters Allied Expeditionary Force] thanking them for their help in the time previous to the invasion of southern France, and the Fourth Platoon of Company B was commended for their work in the Po. Next ?."[143]

Sgt. Grant departed for leave at Rest Camp Roma Italia on June 12, 1945, and returned to duty at Coltano, Italy on June 17.[144]

"I had leave at Rome where I had an audience with the Pope. The Italians must have thought we were crazy because we took shots of cognac with champagne chasers. I visited Pisa where I was able to go to the top of the Leaning Tower of Pisa and ring the bell."[145]

ASSIGNMENT TO THE 57th FIGHTER GROUP, 65th FIGHTER SQUADRON

"On June 22, 1945, in addressing the Battalion this afternoon, Major Martin revealed that most of the men under 84 points will be transferred out of the Battalion and men from other outfits with over 85 points will be in."[146]

A point system was developed to determine which soldiers went home first at the end of WWII. Points were awarded based on the total time a soldier had been in the service, the amount of time spent overseas, and the amount of battle experience based on the number of commendations they had received such as bronze battle stars, silver stars, and others. Soldiers with 85 points or more would go home first. Soldiers with 85 points or more were being transferred into the 594th while those with less than 85 were transferred out. Ultimately the 594th would be sent home. Sgt. Grant only had 76 points, so he was transferred to the 57th Fighter Group, 65th Fighter Squadron.[147]

"I did not have enough points to go home so I was assigned to 57th Fighter Group which was going to be sent straight through to Korea to support the bombers for the attack on Japan because they needed a Morse Code crew chief. But, for some of us if they had enough points, you would be through with the service because we just had the Japanese now. And, if you were lucky and had the right amount of numbers. I think it was eighty-five points you had to have or more, to guarantee you to go back to the states. You won't have to go to the Pacific, unless your particular thing, that you did in the Army or Air Force or Signal Corp, whatever you were in, they needed you. And they

---

[143] Draft text at end of the Diary of the 594th Aircraft Warning Battalion.
[144] 594th, Rpt Co A Morning Reports for June 13, 1945, and June 17, 1945, respectively.
[145] Story told by Stanley Grant.
[146] 594th War Diary, Headquarters and Plotting Co, June, 1945, 594th War Diary, Co A, November, 1944
[147] 65th Fighter Squadron, Morning Report, July 5, 1945

happened to be from our platoon, radar platoon; the Fifty-seventh Fighter Group was going to Korea. The fighter group was going to give protection to bombers that would fly over Japan. So, they needed out of our unit a Morse code crew chief, that was my number, a head cook, [and] another radar unit man. So, we were pulled out of our unit and assigned to Fifty-seventh Group. At the time we were in the Po Valley Italy. That's where the war ended, and we got assigned to the Fifty-seventh Group... was reorganizing in Naples and from Naples was going to go straight through to Korea and cross two oceans in one trip and we got acquainted with the new members of the Fifty-seventh Fighter Group."[148]

On June 24th, 1945 "Early this morning the group of men transferred to the 57th Fighter Group departed for their new station at Grosseto, Italy.'[149],[150]

"When we left the 594th those who were staying gave us a hard time. They said they were going home' and we were going to have to fight the war in the Pacific."[151]

THE 65th FIGHTER SQUADRON MOVES TO NAPLES

"Earlier on June 6, 1945, the 65th Fighter Squadron was alerted for a move which would redeploy the group direct to the Pacific. On June 23rd, orders came through relieving all the old men, and reassigning them to organizations returning to the states. On June 26th, many of the old men left for their organizations, and replacements were slowly coming in to the 65th.[152]

The first of July 1945 finds us with many new men to take up were the old left off. July 5, 1945, we were still waiting and wondering when we are going to move. On July 10, 1945, orders came through that we would move on or about the 14th. We finally will be getting underway and our next job. Preparations for the move to Naples are underway."[153]

"We boarded the train on July 14, 1945, for Naples late at night and as expected there were no lights on the train. We stumbled around in the darkness trying to find seats, and after much confusion, we finally managed to settle down in our seats."[154]

---

[148] Recorded interviews for grade school projects by Stanley Grant's granddaughter, Jennifer Grant, and his Grandson, Michael Johnson
[149] 594th War Diary, June 1945
[150] 65th Fighter Squadron, War Diary, June 1945
[151] Story told by Stanley Grant.
[152] 65th Fighter Squadron, War Diary, June 1945.
[153] 65th Fighter Squadron, War Diary, July 1945
[154] 65th Fighter Squadron, War Diary, July 1945

"Our train pulled out of Grosseto at 0030 hours on July 15, 1945, and our journey to Naples was underway. Everyone was quite comfortable in our wooden compartments. It was apparent to all there wouldn't be much sleep on the train. After a stop in Rome for breakfast, the train continued on its way, and at approximately 2000 hours we arrived in Bagnoli, Italy, and boarded trucks to our new home – Long live the Italian railway systems. A thousand feet up and a thousand feet down. Tomorrow when it is light, we shall be able to judge our surroundings. On July 16, 1945, we see that our new home is the center of an old and dead, we hope, volcano [This is the caldera of the Campi Fiegrei super volcano]. Dust reigns supreme and the heat is queen. The combination is hard to beat. Hope our boat comes soon!"[155]

NAPLES CAMP[156]

WAITING TO LEAVE FOR THE PACIFIC THEATRE

"Processing is underway and as soon as it is over, we hope we leave this place. Life here is more-or-less normal that is if you can stand the dust and heat. Enlisted men are getting passes into Naples every day. A recreation bus leaves every afternoon for the Italian Coney Island where swimming and beer are the main sources of

---

[155] 65th Fighter Squadron, War Diary, July 1945.
[156] 57th Fighter Group, Photographs by James C. "Wabbit" Hare, www.57thfightergroup.org

recreation. Dust and heat, we can say one for this old volcano, it cools off wonderfully in the evenings and sleeping is a pleasure."[157]

"On July 20, 1945, movies in the dust bowl back of our tents were held this evening. The usual continues: passes to town continues. The 1st of August and still no sign of our ship."[158]

"On August 2, 1945, we were alerted this morning at 0800 hours that in a day or two we should be on our way. The name of our ship is the "Sea Owl," and is supposed to be a fair ship. On August 4, 1945, everything is set to go. Hope we leave tomorrow!"[159]

"On August 5 we were told that "Tomorrow …… sometime in the morning….. the Fifty-Seventh Fighter Squadron will board the USAT "Sea Owl" at Naples harbor for a 15,000 mile voyage to the Pacific Theater of Operations.

That was the name given out this afternoon at 1330 hours …… at a formation of all enlisted men of the outfit. After reveille at 0800 hours, the men will eat, return to their tents for final packing of their personal belongings, and wait for the order to load on trucks for their last overland ride for several weeks to come. First stop for the ship, ………, will be at Panama, where the GIs will be permitted to stretch their legs on short passes in one of the Canal Zone's cities."[160]

LEAVING NAPLES AND ENROUTE TO THE PACIFIC

"On August 6, 1945, "Japs here we come. Today we leave for the Pacific and write *finis* to our role in the Mediterranean Theatre. Our job here is finished, and in the days to come we shall start schooling ourselves for our part against our one remaining foe. Good luck to all!"[161]

"We left staging Area #3, Naples, Italy, at 1030 for the docks and boarded the (SS) Sea Owl immediately upon arrival……"[162]

---

[157] 65th Fighter Squadron, War Diary, July 1945.
[158] 65th Fighter Squadron, War Diary, July 1945, and 65th Fighter Squadron, War Diary, August 1945.
[159] 65th Fighter Squadron, War Diary, August 1945.
[160] 66th Fighter Squadron, War Diary, August 1945. Extensive extracts are taken from the 66th Fighter Squadron War Diary because they provide the best description of life on the Sea Owl.
[161] 65th Fighter Squadron, War Diary, August 1945.
[162] 65th Fighter Squadron, War Diary, August 1945.

"We boarded a brand new troopship making its maiden voyage and set on it, headed for Korea…. we had a few thousand guys on the boat, and it was a brand new one. The first time I went over I crossed over on a freighter in the hold of a freighter. This one was spanking brand new troop ship just finished working for a couple of years. So, we were riding first class going over."[163]

"The seemingly interminable waiting period is over. At 1030 hours, after an early breakfast followed by last packing and policing details, the [squadron] threw its collective body onto two-and-a-half ton trucks and negotiated the final drive through the vine-boarded dirt road from Bagnoli to Naples. Arriving at the port's pier 9, GIs, perspiring under the burden of their heavy equipment, were served donuts and lemonade by the Red Cross.

Then came the moment for which the men have been waiting since the end of hostilities in Europe on May 12th the order to for embarkation. As their names were called in time-honored army custom, the squadron members mounted the gangplank and made their precarious ascent without incident. Once aboard, they moved into Compartment "D", second deck in Hatch Two, Forward.

For the men of the [squadron] together with those of the other squadrons of the Group, the ship's mess offered a light, noontime snack of tomato soup ---the first fresh broth in years---and equally fresh apple.

Throughout the early afternoon hours troops of other Pacific-destined units boarded the Sea Owl, while those already on the transport lounged along the boat-deck or explored the various sections of the craft that is to be their floating GI home for the next month and a half.

Lines were cast off at 1400 hours, and with a few Italian dock stewards watching idly from the pier, the Sea Owl was tugged from its berth. The ever-present lucid Neapolitan skies glistened overhead as the ship glided out to the open sea, its rails jam-packed with troops seeking a last nostalgic glimpse of the Iberian Pennisula.

There was no elation, no cheering, no shouting as the sweeping bay of Naples and, later shores of MTO gradually blurred into the indistinct blue haze of the horizon. There was, strangely, no melancholy or gloom, either. Only a grim realisation that a rugged job lies ahead for the 57th.[164]

"We heard about the first one [Atomic Bomb] then about 3-4 days later they hit the second one after the first one was dropped. Everyone knew what was going on and, really didn't know that this bomb did more damage than it was expected to do.

---

[163] Story told by Stanley Grant.
[164] 66th Fighter Squadron, War Diary, August, 1945

Japanese were surprised, too. They weren't quitting, but after the second one like that it destroyed miles of people in every direction. They knew they were finished. Then they didn't have a chance, so they surrendered. Well, it was a big surprise to the rest of the world that something like that would happen.

The atomic bomb wasn't just invented. They had a lot of smart professors put it together....and it was put together and the first reaction... chain reaction they had of it was at the University of Chicago.

I am one of the great was in favor of the atomic bomb. I had a personal thing involved in it. At that time, I was about two years overseas. We were glad that the atomic bomb was dropped."[165]

"We were just a day before we hit the Panama Canal the second bomb was dropped on Japan and the war was over. So, what were they going to do with us on the boat now? They turned the ship around and docked in Boston Harbor".[166]

TROOP SHIP USS SEA OWL ITALY 1945

---

[165] Recorded interviews for grade school projects by Stanley Grant's granddaughter, Jennifer Grant, and his Grandson, Michael Johnson
[166] Story told by Stanley Grant.

"The troop ship was brand new and this was its maiden voyage. The ship I took to North Africa was a freighter."[167]

SOLDIERS BOARDING THE USS SEA OWL

LEAVING NAPLES HARBOR AUGUST 1945[168]

---

[167] Recorded interviews for grade school projects by Stanley Grant's granddaughter, Jennifer Grant, and his Grandson, Michael Johnson
[168] 57th Fighter Group, Photographs by James C. "Wabbit" Hare, www.57thfightergroup.org

SUNSET FIRST DAY AT SEA[169]

Sgt. Grant was transferred from the Signal Corps to the Army Air Force.[170]

August 7: "Day was spent getting organized and acquainted with the Ship."[171]

"Transport life began this morning for the squadron. Breakfast, as well as the meals that followed, were more than just a partaking food on this crowded troop carrier…. they were more quasi-adventures. Chow lines waved like snake-like over all the upper spaces on deck, in and through and around hatches and latrines, up and down and in between ladders and stairs. Two hours was the average time spent waiting for food. The rest of the daylight hours, the GIs idled axially, topside, sunning themselves, playing cards, hugging the rail scanning the horizon for the last sight of the mainland, which under the mid-afternoon slipped into nothingness."[172]

---

[169] 57th Fighter Group, Photographs by James C. "Wabbit" Hare, www.57thfightergroup.org
[170] 65th Fighter Squadron, Morning Report, August 6, 1945
[171] 65th Fighter Squadron, Morning Report, August 7, 1945
[172] 65th Fighter Squadron, War Diary, July 1945.

August 8: "A few men became slightly seasick. No other events."[173]

[The squadron's] enlisted men are living in the second hatch of the Sea Owl, on the second deck below the boat-deck. Bunks of the canvas sack variety are tiered five-deep, with little space between rows. Barracks bags are, for the most part, piled in the open center of the hold.

Altogether, it presents a somewhat disordered cramped sight ---typical of enlisted quarters aboard ships, where all other purposes are only secondary to that of space, or rather lack of space.

Ventilation, however, is better than average here. Cool air filters through pipes overhead, cutting through the dank mass of warm sweat. Nevertheless a large number of the GIs have been sleeping on deck, some of the more fortunate ones having located folding cots.

With the Mediterranean waters peaceful---both in tide and military situation.... no blackout is maintained. Men are permitted to remain on deck, smoking if they like, during the evening. The Sea Owl glides through the calm sea with lights brightly shining -----a marked contrast from the dark, watchful days when the Squadron came overseas, one month and three years ago."[174]

"Easily the most popular feature of the Sea Owl is its wonderful cuisine, the latter word a term that would be euphemistic when generally applied to Army chow. Fresh American food is served daily. For the officers and men of the squadron, it is a noticeable difference from the chow dished out in Italy and Africa. Today for breakfast the men dug in merrily on: half grapefruit: DRY cereal (shredded wheat): scrambled eggs and chopped bacon: coffee, cream, and sugar: marmalade and jelly: and of all things an orange.

Mess kits have been happily scraped for the trip, as the transport is equipped with trays and cups. An efficient, reasonably-pleasure (despite the heat) dining room completes the gastronomic side of the ship. And an agreeable side it is."[175]

August 9: The sea was quite rough today which caused two EM to get seriously Ill. Several others were in bad shape for a while."[176]

---

[173] 65th Fighter Squadron, Morning Report, August 8, 1945
[174] 66th Fighter Squadron, War Diary, August 1945
[175] 66th Fighter Squadron, War Diary, August 1945
[176] 66th Fighter Squadron, War Diary, August 1945

"The waters of the Mediterranean swirled and rolled heavily throughout the day, effecting the first cases of mal-de-mer [seasickness] abroad ship. A few men lined the rail sporadically making their nauseous offerings to Neptune. Others, in the same physiological boat, moaned in their bunks.

Those who could stand the pitching of the Owl attended a movie on open deck, aft of the enlisted men's holds. The film was an entertaining piece starring Monty Woolley and the British entertainer, Gracie Fields.

August 10: "Sea and weather were better today. Everyone apparently in better condition."

Books began to circulate, with the opening of the ship's Special Services Library. Other SS activities included the inauguration of a daily newspaper, and band rehearsals.

Today dusk land appeared to the North---- a hazy line of purple mist, probably Spain, or the Baleares Islands. Gibraltar was passed sometime around midnight tonight."[177]

August 11: "No unusual events other than a rifle inspection which was held to ensure the proper care was being taken of weapons."

---

[177] 66th Fighter Squadron, War Diary, August, 1945

BAND REHEARSAL ON DECK[178]

---

[178] 57th Fighter Group, Photographs by James C. "Wabbit" Hare, www.57thfightergroup.org

ROCK OF GIBRALTAR

"Into the choppy mid-Atlantic ploughed the Sea Owl, while thousands of miles to the west, other American ships were making history. The bombing of Hiroshima on Honshu Island by one history---and atom-smashing bomb---subsequent report that sixty percent of the Jap war center was flattened-----the talk of the transport. Just what it means, or what it would mean, was in the realm of conjecture at this time, but it was especially heartening to this Pacific-bound organization.

Seasickness is still prevalent, although it shows no sign of assuming the proportions of an epidemic. A second showing of last night's film took the special services spotlight on deck tonight."[179]

August 12: "A false peace rumor created quite a furor today and started a small party in the officers mess. It is rumored that two officers with long hair don't have it anymore."[180]

"The stirring news of the last two days----Russia's entry into the Asiatic war and the use of the atomic bomb, coupled with persistent, but unconfirmed contentions that the Japanese are suing for peace---has swept through all the ranks. Rumors, speculations, and wild guesses are making their play from end of the ship to another.

---

[179] 66th Fighter Squadron, War Diary, August, 1945
[180] 65th Fighter Squadron, Morning Report, August 12, 1954

What is to be the future of the 57th Fighter Group? How has the present turn of events affected this shipment? Many a GI lay awake in his bunk tonight, as the motors whirred constantly, these questions hovering in his mind."[181]

August 13: "No unusual events."[182]

"A veil of uncertainty shrouded the international news last night and all of today. Still----almost to the man, the troops aboard the Owl are convinced that the Japs have "had it----that the war is lingering on last desperate breath. All activity aboard ship seems to center about the news. Men cluster around the several loudspeakers in the hatches and on deck, waiting for even the barest scrapes of the developments in the reported-and-denied-and-reported-again statements that Japan has thrown in the proverbial, and much-hoped-for, towel.

But, withal, the Sea Owl is steaming into the soft green waters of the Gulf Stream, plying itself soberly to its set course for Panama. But even while watching the deck shows---musical varieties staged and produced by the enlisted men aboard-----the Army passengers are talking and wondering---and, of course, hoping."[183]

August 14: "War with Japan is over. News was received with great enthusiasm and many bottles appeared out of thin air. It is amazing how the stuff can be obtained so far out at sea."[184]

"It's over. The fantastic, unbelievable, wonderful crazy news that Japan has surrendered is true. There is peace throughout the world today for the first time since 1931.

Over the loudspeaker tonight, the mast of the vessel, graying Merchant Marine man Captain Richard Snow crisply told the troops aboard that the President had announced the end of the greatest armed conflict that the world has ever witnessed. It was stunning, glorious news. The men yelled, danced, capered, clapped each other's backs, sung, screamed, leaped, ran onto deck, laughing, crying-----".... the war is over....over!

When the first shock of the fateful word had passed into a dim realization, the ship buzzed with rumors. Now that the war is over----all over---the rumors whispered,

---

[181] 66th Fighter Squadron, War Diary, August 1945
[182] 65th Fighter Squadron, Morning Report, August 13, 1945
[183] 66th Fighter Squadron, War Diary, August 1945
[184] 65th Fighter Squadron, Morning Report, August 14, 1945

what will happen to us? They have no reason to send us to the Pacific. No reason on earth.[185]

Yet the Sea Owl kept on heading into the sun------westward---unmindful of what had happened. Panama lay two days ahead."[186]

August 15: "Many hangovers were visible today. Our course has been changed and we are now heading for Boston, Mass, USA. Morale is very high."[187]

"Early this morning, at 0630 hours, while breakfast chow lines were taking shape in the half dark, the loudspeaker suddenly crackled:

"Orders have been radioed in, directing that this transport proceed to Boston Harbor, without delay…"

"What followed was a fitting anti-climax to last night's V-J celebrations, only slightly more so. The decks rang with a vibrant cheer that arose after the word "Boston" was heard.

Home is three days away, furloughs, and possibly a discharge for the 80 pointers soon----this now is the prospect for the men of the squadron. In a queer, uncanny chain of stranger-than-fiction-events, the very destiny of hundreds of men and pilots aboard this ship was radically altered.

Only seven short days ago the future looked bleak for the personnel of this squadron. The Pacific and an apparently long, rugged fight was ahead. Then, in the incredible space of a week, that entire horizon was obliterated.

The band rehearsal tonight was something to see, and hear, when compared with the former ones. The men couldn't resist grinning and joking at the least provocation. Home in three days! Oh, God! "[188]

"We were in the middle of the Atlantic Ocean headed for the Panama Canal on our way to the Pacific when Japan surrendered. So, we were diverted to Boston. Guards had to be posted to stop men from throwing equipment overboard." [189]

---

[185] 66th Fighter Squadron, War Diary, August 1945
[186] 66th Fighter Squadron, War Diary, August 1945
[187] 65th Fighter Squadron, Morning Report, August 15, 1945
[188] 66th Fighter Squadron, War Diary, August 1945
[189] Story told by Stanley Grant.

August 16: "No Land in sight. Spirits are very high with everyone wishing this ship was equipped with jet propulsion."[190]

"It was still the same rolling ocean, and no land was yet in sight, but for all the men of the [squadron] cared, it might have been a mass of luxuriant ambrosia or the entrance to the Elysian Fields. The weather was bright and mild, the sky flecked with scattered lacy clouds. Although it was understood that American shores would not become visible for two days, the men couldn't resist hanging alongside the rail, searching for a glimpse of home. An impatient excitement could be felt running through the ship in accentuating waves. No one, it seemed, felt like doing much more than day and night dreaming about his wife or sweetheart or family. The editors of the ship's daily Sea Owl had rushed out an extra on the day of the Jap surrender and then had quietly washed their hands of mimeograph ink, hurled out the paste pots and sunk into happy meditation.

Were before time had rushed past, it now crept miserably along at a caterpillar's pace. Home…. Home…. Home"[191]

August 17: "Weather bad and sea very rough. A few cases of seasickness otherwise everything was normal."[192]

"The day before debarkation at Boston. The happy job of packing up equipment and belongings began, with everyone in an eager frame of mind to complete the task quickly, as if that in itself could draw the GI closer to the New England coast.

At night clandestine trips were made to the railing topside, and tell-tale splashes hinted strongly that the GIs were relieving the barracks and duffle bags of the thousand-odd items that soldiers invariably and inevitably picked up. French and Italian mattresses, footlockers, chests-----all deemed vitally necessary weeks before the trip for life in the Pacific -----were now being surreptitiously dumped overboard. For after all, in a tiny matter of hours, the wonder and comfort of America would be reached.

Time had all but stopped…twenty-four hours never to pass."[193]

---

[190] 65th Fighter Squadron, Morning Report, August 16, 1945
[191] 66th Fighter Squadron, War Diary, August 1945
[192] 65th Fighter Squadron, Morning Report, August 17, 1945
[193] 66th Fighter Squadron, War Diary, August 1945

BOSTON HARBOR, CAMP, MYLES STANDISH, AND DISCHARGE

August 18: "Home at Last! We were met by a boat loaded with WACS, WAVES, and women. It was rumored that there was a large male band also but no one saw them so it has not been confirmed. All the boats in the harbor blew their whistles in salute."[194]

"Today's homecoming for the men aboard the Sea Owl was like something out of newsreels and glamour-war novels. There was no tickertape, no parade, but no one seemed to notice or care. There was too much else to see, and to hear.

"When at about eleven in the morning, the ship steamed past a huge "WELCOME HOME-WELL DONE" sign erected on an island just outside the Port of Boston, a light Army transportation vessel drew up to the starboard. Aboard the smaller craft were crammed a band, WACS, GIs, civilian men, women, WAVES, a soldier costumed as Uncle Sam, and dozens of pretty little creatures, all waving and shouting and cheering. As the OWL was sluggishly tugged into its berth, the numerous ships in the harbor let forth their greeting whistles in a deafening screech." [195]

ARRIVING BOSTON HARBOR[196]

---

[194] 65th Fighter Squadron, Morning Report, August 18, 1945
[195] 66th Fighter Squadron, War Diary, August 1945
[196] 57th Fighter Group, Photographs by James C. "Wabbit" Hare, www.57thfightergroup.org

"Quite a homecoming! After disembarking [at 1200 hours] at Boston Commonwealth Pier we were loaded on a train and left for Camp Myles Standish 30 miles away."[197]

"When I left the ship all I had with me was a small overnight bag. I was a gentlemen soldier. " [198]

"Colors, music, voices, ship's whistles-----all rose in a noisily-blended tone and sight pictures for the troops aboard the transport, making the 18th of August a day never to be forgotten by the men of the [squadron].

Later in the afternoon, when the novelty and excitement had worn off, debarkation took place. Each soldier descending the gangplank stepped through an archway symbolic of home, the personification of Uncle Sam in the guise of a transportation corps T/5, personally greeted each GI with a firm handshake and a "Welcome Home, buddy". In small groups, the gay debarkees were trooped off by WAC guides to wait for the coaches for the ride to the nearby camp. Before train time, the Red Cross came through with donuts and milk-----the old-fashioned kind that come in liquid form.

The jaunt to the reception station, Camp Myles Standish, near Taunton, Mass., was short and comfortable. Just the thrill of traveling in an American train after two years and more of African 40-and-8s and wheeling European second and third class was enough to make the hour long-journey a milestone.

And after the preliminary work of assigning the men to barracks, issuing bedding, and holding a brief (and surprisingly entertaining) orientation lecture, the Squadron dashed off to the Bell Telephone Building for that first call home.

Dinner that day was, itself, notable event. The menu included: pork chops, mashed potatoes, salad with French dressing, peas, cake, ice cream, coffee, milk, iced-water, rolls, coffee, and tons of butter.

The PXs did a thriving business that day from the influx of Americana hungry exterminators. Cokes flowed like wine, along with hair-tonic and shaving lotions of the more fragrant groups. And the pinball machines were tilted that day as rarely before."[199]

---

[197] 65th Fighter Squadron, Morning Report, August 18, 1945
[198] Story told by Stanley Grant.
[199] 66th Fighter Squadron, War Diary, August, 1945

COMMONWEALTH PIER BOSTON

CAMP MYLES STANDISH

"Upon arrival at Camp Myles Standish we were given a brief orientation as to what was to become of us, and then we were fed a first-class meal of steak and fresh milk with all the trimmings. There is no shortage of beer so most of the men made up for lost time. There are no passes granted at this station, so we have to make the most of it here on the post."[200]

August 19 and 20th, "Everyone has been busy trying to get the unit cleared so we can start those 30-day leaves. Have completed our work and are to leave for reception stations some time tomorrow. Permanent personnel at Camp Myles Standish have amazed everyone with their efficiency and willingness to cooperate. They made our stay as short and pleasant as possible."[201]

"Equipment and baggage were trundled off to supply this morning, to be shipped by the government to Drew Field Army Air Base at Tampa, Florida, the assigned assembly area for the [squadron]. The men themselves were busied with the pleasant task of selecting the reception stations nearest their home, stations which would send them on their final way homeward.

Two mail calls were held today, but nobody was particularly interested in letters. Only a few hours lay between the soldier and his loved ones."

Starting this morning, and continuing through the afternoon, men of the squadron pulled out of the railroad station at Camp Standish, enroute to their various reception centers. It had been a long hail, this voyage from Naples to Boston, with the strong scare of a Pacific destination added.

What the future of the squadron and its members would be, no one knew as the men boarded troop trains for the next-to-last lap on their homecoming journey. A small percentage of …..personnel had already been sent to the Separation Center for discharge under the 80-points ruling.

But whatever the outcome, for the present only the thoughts of home prevailed, and a determination to remember as little of the Army and Italy and the war as possible during the coming thirty days.[202]

August 21-22nd, "The Squadron Commander and two enlisted men are leaving for our assembly area at Drew Field, Tampa, Florida. Departed by RR [railroad] at 1000 hrs for Drew Field.[203] All personnel have left Camp Myles Standish for reception

---

[200] 65th Fighter Squadron, War Diary, August 1945.
[201] 65th Fighter Squadron, War Diary, August 1945.
[202] 66th Fighter Squadron, War Diary, August 1945
[203] 65th Fighter Squadron, Morning Report, August 21, 1945

stations...."[204] "Auth 30 days RRR Boston POE dd 20 Aug 45."[205] [Authorized 30 days Rest, Recovery, and Relaxation at Boston Port of Entry as of August 20, 1945]

"So, they still did not know what to do with us, so they sent assigned everybody back to the state or city where you were drafted. We had boys from all over the country in our unit. So, I went back to Camp Grant. So, they still did not know what to do with us. So, we had plenty of time coming because we were supposed to get thirty days vacation time in the service every twelve months you put in. We all had 60 or 90 days coming. So, I got two months vacation time to go back home and by that time they'll know what to do with us. Well later was in the first two weeks in November and I was discharged from the service."[206]

August 21 through 18 October

"While the officers and men of the [squadron] were relaxing throughout the country in the luxury of 30-day leaves, measures were being taken in Washington by the Army chiefs to affect a rapid demobilization, and a sweeping reorganization of the military, now that the war had come to an abrupt end.

The 57th Fighter Group, with its component squadrons, was ordered deactivated at Drew Field-----its services no longer required. And separation centers began to mushroom coast to coast to discharge the outgoing flux of personnel. First the critical ASR was lowered to 80 then to 70, and finally, a droppage to 60 on the First of November was promised.

All these re[ductions] gradually but surely hacked away at the squadron. The majority of men, in the high point brackets, received discharges after their 45-day leaves. The 60-pointers were sent home again, there to wait the lowering of the score in November.

So only a skeleton crew of [squadron] members showed up at Drew Field. Of these even less were assigned to Detachment X, the base's clearinghouse for de-activated units, to complete the administrative dismantlement of the group. The others were transferred to other organizations throughout the Third Air Force.

It is only a matter of days now until the squadron and group will send in their last morning report. The 57th Fighter Group, thrice winner of the Distinguished Unit Badge in three years of combat overseas, is about to be officially retired.

---

[204] 65th Fighter Squadron, War Diary, August 1945.
[205] 65th Fighter Squadron, Morning Report, August 21, 1945
[206] Recorded interviews for grade school projects by Stanley Grant's granddaughter, Jennifer Grant, and his Grandson, Michael Johnson

It would not be maudlin to say that few members of the [squadron,] past, present, or perhaps in the future, will never forget the ....or "Calling.........Jackpot".[207]

Sgt. GRANT AND HELEN GRANT CHICAGO OCTOBER 1945

---

[207] 66th Fighter Squadron, War Diary, August 1945

As noted in the 65th Morning Report of Oct. 23, 1945: On October 14, 1945, Sgt. Grant was assigned and transferred to the separation center at Camp Grant Illinois.

"They did not know what to do with us, so they gave us thirty days leave. I went home. Then they gave us fifteen days additional leave. Then they told us to report to the location where we had entered the service to be discharged. So, I had to travel to Camp Grant to be discharged".[208]

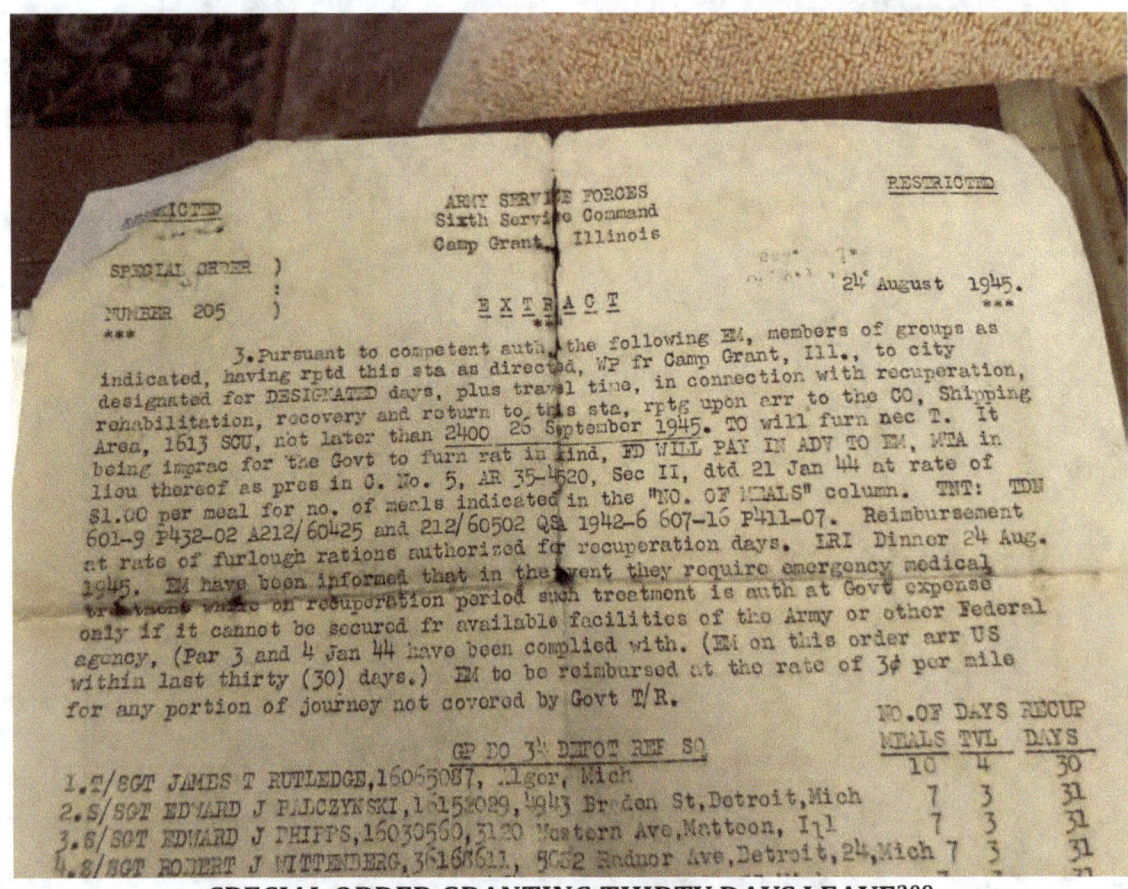

SPECIAL ORDER GRANTING THIRTY DAYS LEAVE[209]

---

[208] Story told by Stanley Grant.
[209] Photograph provided by Marilyn Johnson, Stanley Grant's daughter.

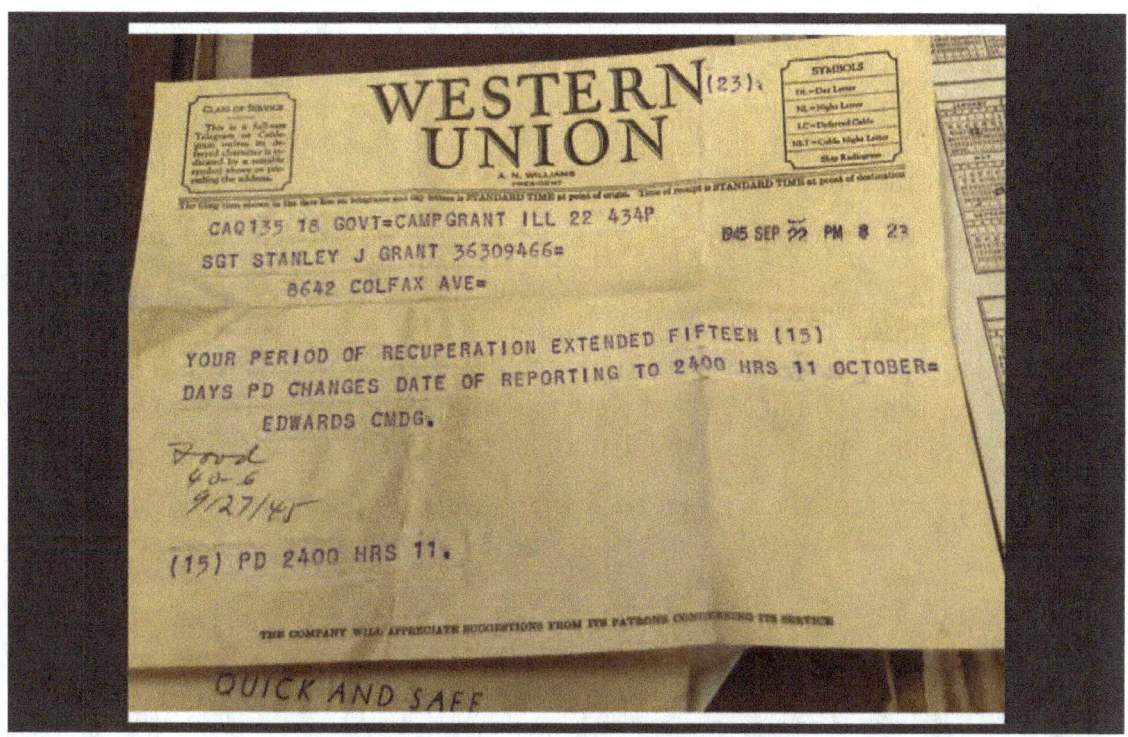

TELEGRAM EXTENDING LEAVE FIFTEEN DAYS[210]

"I was back home in late August 1945 months ahead of the guys of the 594th who gave us a hard time about how they were going home while we were going to fight in the Pacific. It took them months to get home because there were so many men that needed to come home, and there was not enough transport to do so in a timely way."[211]

"When I got home, I was treated Like a Prince! Everybody was glad to see me.

I did not see any changes in town, family…everything back home was going along.

Oh, we were going out and meeting everybody. There was always somebody coming in from the old gang and making the city shows and dance places. We figured we missed all that had time to try to catch up.

Everybody seemed to go along go back into their old routine again…it was all over. Mine changed because I was an apprentice butcher. I got out of that…got an

---

[210] Photograph provided by Marilyn Johnson, Stanley Grant's daughter.
[211] Story told by Stanley Grant.

apprenticeship as a carpenter. That's how it changed my life."[212] *"I never thought of myself as a hero."*[213]

Sgt. Grant was discharged from the Army of the United States (AUS) on October 19 1945 at Camp Grant Illinois. [214]

AFTER THE WAR

After the war, Stanley Grant became an apprentice carpenter and received his carpenter's journeyman's certificate on October 1, 1948. At first, he worked on building new houses. About 1950, he went to work for the City of Chicago Board of Education, and he remained in that job until his retirement in the early 1980's.

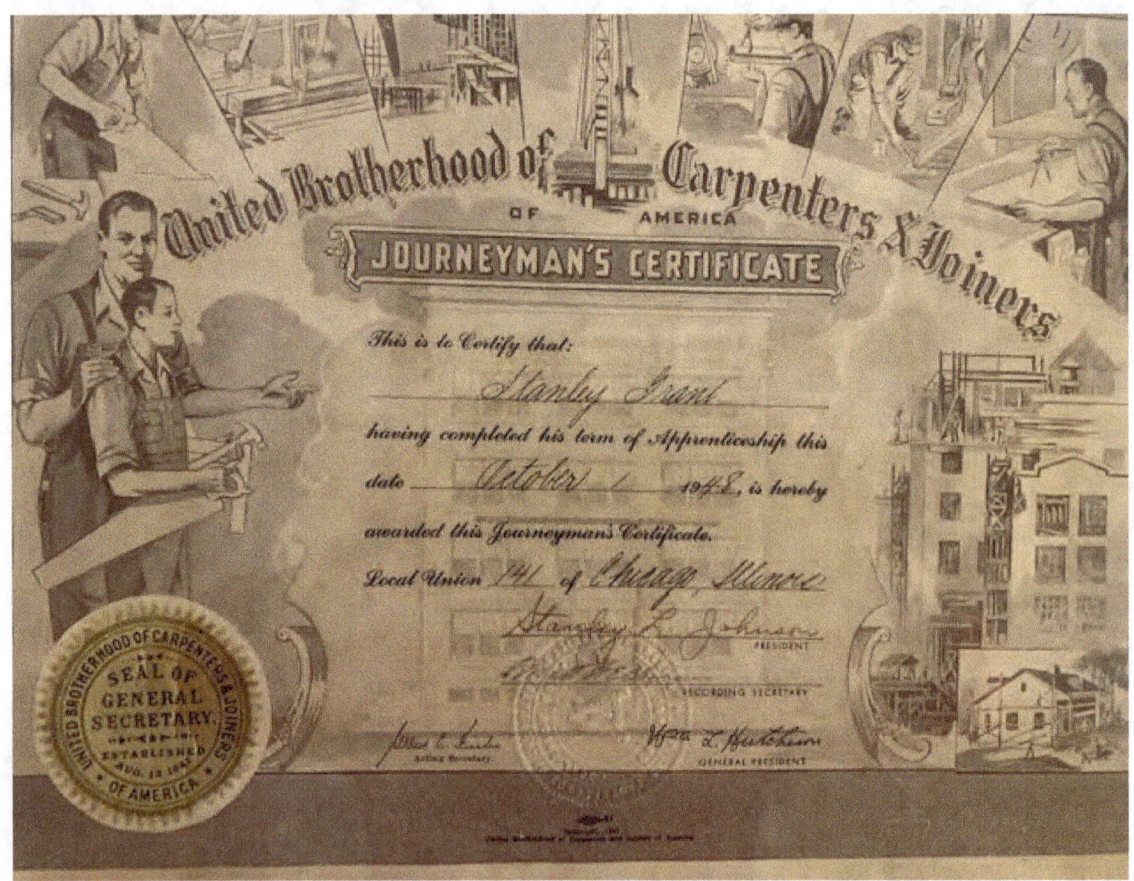

STANLEY GRANT'S CARPENTER JOURNEYMAN'S CERTIFICATE

---

[212] Recorded interviews for grade school projects by Stanley Grant's granddaughter, Jennifer Grant, and his grandson, Michael Johnson
[213] Recorded interviews for grade school projects by Stanley Grant's granddaughter, Jennifer Grant, and his grandson, Michael Johnson
[214] Enlisted Record and Report of Separation and Honorable Discharge, Stanley J. Grant, 10 October 1945

In spite of hardships growing up during the Depression and serving overseas, he had a positive view of life and what he had. He enjoyed his job and family. He and Helen saw a better future for their four children through education. One became a chemical engineer, another a lawyer, and two are pharmacists. Helen passed in 1992, and Stanley passed in 2006.

STANLEY GRANT MILITARY RECORD

Sgt Grant's discharge paper states that:

1. He qualified for: Marksman (MM) Rifle

2. His Military Occupational Specialty (MOS) and number were: Radio Operator 766.

3. He participated in the following Battles and Campaigns: Rome-Arno, North Apennines, and Po Valley.

4. He was awarded the following decorations and citations: European-African-Middle Eastern Theater Ribbon with Bronze Battle Star, 1 Service stripe, 3 Overseas Bars, and the Good Conduct Medal.

5. He was issued the "Ruptured Duck" lapel button, which indicated that he was honorably discharged from the military service of the United States.

SGT GRANT DISCHARGE PAPER

His discharge paper was incorrect and incomplete because he should have received three bronze battle stars: one for each of the three campaigns in which he participated, the American Theater Ribbon for the time he spent in the Continental

United States, and the World War II Victory Medal. He also qualified as a marksman (MM) Carbine as indicated by the attachment to his MM badge.

A request was sent to the Air Force to correct Sgt. Grant's service record. The Air Force issued a DD FORM 215, CORRECTION TO DD FORM 214 which stated "FROM: "European-African-Middle Eastern Theater Ribbon with/ bronze battle star" TO "European-African-Middle Eastern Theater Ribbon with/ three bronze service stars." ADD: American Champaign Medal, World War II Victory Medal."

SGT GRANT'S GOOD CONDUCT MEDAL[215]

---

[215] Photograph provided by Michael Johnson, grandson

SGT GRANT'S RIBBONS[216]

---

[216] Photograph provided by Michael Johnson, grandson

SGT GRANT'S MARKSMAN BADGE[217]

---

[217] Photograph provided by Michael Johnson, grandson

STANLEY GRANT WWII TIMELINE AND LOCATIONS 1941-1945

Date	WWII Event	Stanley Grant Location
December 7, 1941	Japanese Bomb Pearl Harbor	8642 Colfax Ave, Chicago, Ill
January 5, 1942	Stanley Grant inducted into Army	Camp Grant, Rockford, Ill
January 7, 1942	Pvt. Grant arrives Fort Dix	Fort Dix, NJ
January 31, 1942	Pvt. Grant assigned to 569th Signal Aircraft Warning Company (SAW), Frontier	Fort Story, VA
May 8, 1942	Pvt. Grant Assigned to Kitty Hawk Detachment of 569th SAW	Kitty Hawk (KH), NC
May 21, 1942	Pvt. Grant on Furlough	Chicago, Ill
May 27, 1942	Pvt. Grant returns to Duty at Fort Story	Fort Story, VA
June 11, 1942	Pvt. Grant returns to Duty at KH	KH, NC
Sept. 1, 1942	Pvt. Grant on Duty at Keystone Radio School	Hollidaysburg, PA
Nov. 5, 1942	Pvt. Grant promoted to Technician Fifth Grade (T/5)	Hollidaysburg, PA
Nov. 8, 1942	US troops land in North Africa	
Nov. 21, 1942	T/5 Grant married Helen Michalak	Chicago, Ill
Nov. 27, 1942	T/5 Grant graduates from Keystone Radio School	Hollidaysburg, PA
Dec. 1, 1942	T/5 Grant returns to Duty at KH	KH, NC
Dec. 17, 1942	T/5 Grant on furlough	Chicago, ILL
Dec. 27, 1942	T/5 Grant returns to Duty at KH	KH, NC
Jan. 1, 1943	T/5 Grant promoted to Sergeant	KH, NC
March 20, 1943	Sgt, Grant on Furlough	Chicago, Ill
March 27, 1943	Sgt. Grant returns to Duty at KH	KH, NC
May 13, 1943	German troops surrender in North Africa	
July 10, 1943	Allies land in Sicily	
Aug. 17, 1943	All Axis withdrawn from Sicily	
Sept. 3, 1943	Allies land in southern Italy	
Sept. 28, 1943	Allies capture Naples	
Nov. 16, 1943	Sgt. Grant Assigned to 594th SAW Battalion (Bn) at Fort Dix Further assigned to Company A, 2nd Platoon	Fort Dix, NJ
Dec. 11, 1943	Sgt. Grant on DS at Bradley Field	Windsor Locks, CT
Dec. 17, 1943	Sgt. returns to Duty at Fort Dix	Fort Dix, NJ
Jan. 4, 1944	594th SAW Bn arrives at Camp Patrick Henry	Newport News, VA
Jan. 12, 1944	Company A, 594th SAW Bn boards Liberty Ship Cornelius Hartnett	Hampton Roads, VA
Jan. 13, 1944	Cornelius Hartnett anchored in Channel near Hampton Roads	Hampton Roads, VA

Jan. 14, 1944	Cornelius Hartnett departs for Unknown destination	Hampton Roads, VA
Feb. 1, 1944	Cornelius Hartnett arrives at Oran, Algeria	Oran, Algeria
Feb. 3, 1944	594th Bn quartered at Mediterranean Base Section, Staging Area 2	Oran, Algeria
Feb. 16, 1944	594th Bn arrived at Port of Mostaganem, Algeria	Mostaganem, Algeria
March 28, 1944	Company A, 2nd Platoon at Ouilles, Algeria for operational training	Ouilles, Algeria
May 24, 1944	Company A, 2nd and 3rd Platoons departed Oran for Sardinia/Corsica on French cruiser Emil Bertin	Oran, Algeria
May 25, 1944	Company A, 2nd and 3rd Platoons on detached service with the 325th Fighter Control Squadron (FCS)	Sardinia/Corsica
June 6, 1944	Allies capture Rome	Corsica/Sardinia
June 7, 1944	Allies land in Normandy	Corsica/Sardinia
June, 1944	325th FCS base of operations set up at Calvi, Corsica	Calvi, Corsica
June 22, 1944	Company A, 2nd Platoon on Duty near Catteraggie, Corsica	Chisohaccia, Corsica
Aug. 5, 1944	Allies reach Arno River in Italy	Chisohaccia, Corsica
Aug. 25, 1944	Allies liberate Paris	Chisohaccia, Corsica
Sept. 10, 1944	Company A, 2nd and 3rd Platoons released form DS with 325th FCS	Bastia, Corsica
Mid Oct., 1944	Company A, 2nd and 3rd Platoons arrived at Pisa Air Base	Pisa, Italy
Nov. 1944	Company A, 2nd and 3rd Platoons Relocated to Coltano, Italy	Coltano, Italy
Late Nov. 1944	Main party of 594th Bn arrived at Coltano, Italy	Coltano, Italy
End of Nov. 1944	Company A, 2nd Platoon operating at Montanero, Italy	Montanero, Italy
Dec. 16, 1944	Patton relieves Bastogne	
Mar 24, 1945	Company A, 2nd Platoon moved to Castelfranca, Italy	Castelfranca, Italy
April 4, 1945	Allies break through North Apennines into Po River valley	
May 2, 1945	Allies capture Northern Italy. Germany surrenders.	
May 8, 1945	VE Day	
End of May	594th Bn Platoons back at Coltano, Italy	Coltano, Italy

June 12, 1945	Sgt. Grant on leave at Rest Camp Roma Italia	Rome, Italy
June 17, 1945	Sgt. Grant back on Duty at Coltano	Coltano, Italy
June 24, 1945	Sgt. Grant transferred to 57th Fighter Group, 65th Fighter Squadron at Grossetto Air Base	Grossetto, Italy
July 14, 1945	57th FG Boarded train for Naples	Grossetto, Italy
July 15, 1945	57th FG arrived at Bagnoli and and transferred to Naples Camp	Bagnoli, Italy
Aug. 6, 1945	Atomic bomb on Hiroshima 57th FG left Staging Area #3 for the docks and boarded the SS Sea Owl and immediately got underway to Pacific. Sgt. Grant was transferred from the Signal Corps of the Army Ground Force to the Army Air Force	Naples, Italy
Aug. 9, 1945	Atomic bomb on Nagasaki	
Aug. 14, 1945	Heard the News of Japan's Surrender. Sea Owl diverted to Boston	At sea
Aug. 18, 1945	Arrived at Boston Harbor. Traveled by train to Camp Myles Standish	Commonwealth Pier Camp Myles Standish Near Taunton, MA
Aug. 20, 1945	All personnel departed Camp Myles Standish. Given 45 days RRR. Sgt. Grant returned to Camp Grant and then Chicago, Ill	Camp Myles Standish to Chicago, Ill
Oct. 14, 1945	Sgt. Grant returned to Camp Grant for discharge	Camp Grant, Rockford, Ill
Oct. 19, 1945	Sgt. Grant discharged from the Army	Camp Grant, Rockford, Ill. Went home to 7133 Ingleside Ave, Chicago, Ill

ADDITIONAL PHOTOGRAPHS
ON DUTY

STAN MANEUVERS KITTY HAWK 1942

STAN KITTY HAWK 1942 "I LOOK LIKE A BOSS HERE, DON'T I?"

STAN K.P. KITTY HAWK 1942 "ME ON K.P. NOTICE THE DOG TAGS AROUND MY NECK"

STAN ON GUARD DUTY KITTY HAWK 1942

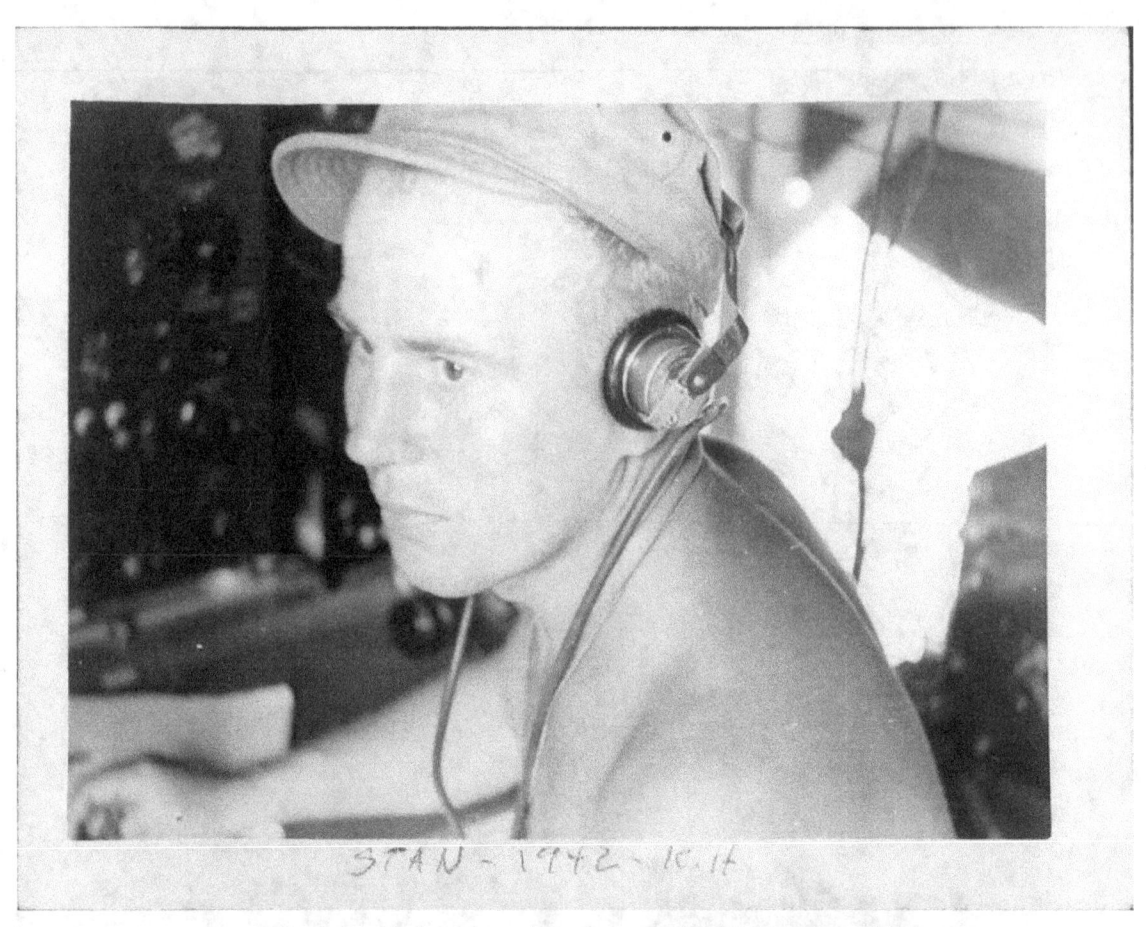

STAN AT RADIO KITTY HAWK 1942

STAN SENDING MORSE CODE KITTY HAWK 1943

MOVING OUT ON AN OVERNIGHT KITTY HAWK 1943

GAS MASK DRILL KITTY HAWK 1943

STAN KITTY HAWK 1943

STAN KITTY HAWK NORTH CAROLINA 1943

**OUR COOKS DECEMBER 1942 KITTY HAWK
BOTTOM ROW: LICHERT (PA), MELLONI (PA), BELU (NJ)
TOP ROW: CALABRESE (NY), KOBUS (MESS SGT, CHICAGO),
LENZA (CHICAGO)**

OFF DUTY

VIRGINIA BEACH SPRING 1942 MYSKER, STAN

STAN, HOMEMADE WASH BASIN STAND – SHOWER IN REAR 1942

STAN NAGS HEAD WOODS

DUCK ELIZABETH CITY NC 1942

STAN MANTEO NC 1942

CHURCH ON BEACH KITTY HAWK 1943

EASTER 1943 KITTY HAWK

ALTER AT KITTY HAWK CHURCH 1943 EASTER

DOGWOOD BLOSSOMS EASTER KITTY HAWK 1943

BLACKIE CAMP DOG

HELEN VISITS KITTY HAWK

HELEN AND STAN KITTY HAWK 1943

ALICE AND HELEN KITTY HAWK 1943

ALICE AND HELEN WASHING HAIR KITTY HAWK 1943

STAN AND HELEN SQUIREL HUNTING AT KITTY HAWK 1943

STAN AND HELEN AT CEMETERY KITTY HAWK 1943

HELEN AND STAN VIRGINIA BEACH 1943

HELEN VIRGINIA BEACH 1943

HELEN AND STAN VIRGINIA BEACH 1943

CAMPING TRIP

STAN START OF THREE-DAY CAMPING TRIP 1943

STAN AND BLACKIE CAMPING TRIP 1943

STAN START OF CAMPING TRIP WITH DUCK

CAMP NORTH CAROLINA 1943

DUCK ALBERMARLE SOUND NORTH CAROLINA 1943

STAN FISHING NORTH CAROLINA 1943

STAN FISHING TRIP 1943

STAN COOKING FISH NORTH CAROLINA 1943

WILD PIGS FISHING TRIP NORTH CAROLINA 1943

STAN RETURNING FROM FISHING TRIP NORTH CAROLINA 1943

HISTORY OF THE WW II EAST COAST AIR DEFENSE NETWORK

Development of Radar

Prior to World War II the Air Force was primarily focused on offense because of the view that effective interception depended chiefly on luck, and due to oceans and distance there was no possibility of an immediate attack on United States.[218] "As a result, the United States lagged behind in the development of radar which would deprive attacking air forces the advantage of surprise." [219]

The British, much closer to their potential enemies, pushed their radar program so that by 1939 a chain of stations guarded their coasts. And in 1940, British scientists developed the resonant cavity magnetron a powerful device which made microwave radar practical.[220]

The British also developed a very high frequency (VHF) radio for ground-to-air and plane-to-plane communications that was superior to the high frequency (HF) radios used by U. S. Services. [221]

" The revolutionary potential of these devices added more stimulus to a growing concern within the Air Corps for its air defense responsibilities." [222]

By 1939 the Army prototype mobile radar, SCR-270, with a range of over 120 miles, and its fixed-installation companion, SCR-271, were ready for tests, but operational models were not available for use until 1940 [223]

---

[218] The Army Air Forces in World War II, Men, Men and Planes, Volume VI, Edited by W. F. Craven and J. L. Cate, University of Chicago Press, Chicago, Illinois, 1955. p. 80.
[219] *Ibid.*, p. 82.
[220] *Ibid.*, p. 83
[221] *Ibid.*, p. 84
[222] *Ibid.*, p. 84
[223] *Ibid.*, p. 83

Development of Continental Air Defense

The War Department activated the Air Defense Command on February 26, 1940, with the mission to study the problem of air defense. [224]

"The first major assignment of the new command was the operation of an air defense net in connection with First Army's 1940 maneuvers near Watertown, Connecticut."[225]

"The first full-scale test of the air defenses of a vital urban area of the United States was carried out….. in January 1941. The warning service, easily the most elaborate yet attempted in America, was organized in a sector reaching along the east coast from New York to Boston. The results convinced the Air Corps that control of interception from regional centers was practical."[226]

"In March 1941, four air commands designated the First through Fourth Air Forces were established within the Eastern, Central, Southern, and Western United States, respectively. Each air force created its own interceptor command with direct control of the air defense units in its area, including aircraft warning services and antiaircraft units." [227]

As plans took shape in the spring of 1941, the responsible commands had a deadline of August 1 to establish a series of radar stations for early warning of an enemy's approach by sea. Volunteer observers had to be recruited, organized, and trained by the thousands for tracking the movement of planes over land. Information centers to receive and filter the reports from radar and observation posts to be located, with facilities for air force controllers who would issue orders to alert all defense agencies, both passive and active. [228]

"The radar stations, to manned exclusively by military units, required large numbers of trained technicians and the installation of complex equipment. More immediately, the choice of the sites proved to be a time-consuming process in itself." Once approved, "the District Engineer acquired the property, temporarily by right of trespass and permanently by lease." [229]

"The goal was a chain of radar installations along both coasts, with breaks of approximately seventy miles between stations. But at time of Pearl Harbor there were only eight stations fully ready for operations: two on the east coast and six along the Pacific." [230]

---

[224] *Ibid.*, p. 84-85
[225] Ibid., p. 85
[226] Ibid., p. 85
[227] *Ibid.*, p. 86
[228] *Ibid.*, p. 87
[229] *Ibid.*, p. 89
[230] *Ibid.*, p. 89

During my research for this book, I learned a lot about the deployment of radar on the northeast coast of the United States during WWII. For those who are interested, I organized the following short history of the air defenses along the eastern board of the United States during WWII

Beginning of Aircraft Warning Companies

The task of organizing the air defense along the Eastern Seaboard defense was assigned to the First Fighter Command.[231] "The Signal Companies attached to the First Fighter Command were charged with the task of: Obtaining information of seaward air traffic by means of Radar stations along the coast; transmission of this information, and reports of overland flights from a network of Ground Observers Spotter Posts stretching into the interior, by means of telephone communications to Filter Centers and Information Centers; and the plotting of these flights on Filter and Operation Boards for identification or, if proved enemy, for interception by friendly aircraft.[232]

One of these Signal Companies was the 609th Signal Aircraft Warning Company, Regional attached to the Norfolk Fighter Wing.

"The story of how this company eventually became designated the [609th] Signal Aircraft Warning Company, Regional is one of constant organization and reorganization, of changing personnel and size of units to fit the newly discovered needs of an expanding system."[233]

"Its origin may be traced to the first aircraft warning companies on the Eastern Seaboard. The following organizations comprised the aircraft warning set-up prior to the subsequent expansion of that service:

First Aircraft Warning Company
First Operations Company (AW)
Second Aircraft Warning Company
Second Operations Company (AW)
Signal Headquarters and Headquarters Company (AW)
505th Signal Operations Company (AW)"[234]

---

[231] Unit history of the 601st Signal Aircraft Warning Company, National Archives, College Park, Maryland. p. 1
[232] *Ibid.*, p. 1
[233] *Ibid.*, p. 2
[234] *Ibid.*, p. 3

The First Aircraft Warning Company

"The First Aircraft Warning Company was activated sometime early in 1940 at Ft. Monmouth, New Jersey. Personnel was recruited from reception centers and very carefully selected. The Cadre was composed of regular Army men. Shortly after activation personnel of the First Aircraft Warning Company moved to Watertown, New York, for maneuvers, making their headquarters temporarily in Pine Camp. Upon completion of maneuvers personnel of the First Aircraft Warning Company moved to Manorville, Long Island, in the latter part of April 1941, for further aircraft warning training, using SCR's 268 and 270-B. These maneuvers lasted for approximately one month. Because of overcrowded conditions existing at Ft. Monmouth at this time, the First Aircraft Warning Company was compelled to break off maneuvers and return to Ft. Monmouth in order to pack and change their headquarters to Camp Mills, Mitchel Field. This camp had been a former World War I installation and was in a state of disuse up to the time of its occupation, in the Spring of 1941. During the period when the First Aircraft Warning Company was changing stations to Camp Mills, the Second Aircraft Warning Company, which had been activated at Mitchel Field from a cadre taken from the First Aircraft Warning Company, took over and operated the SCR-268 units already set up. The First Aircraft Warning Company built up Camp Mills from nothing but rows of winterized tents to a permanent installation. In July 1941 a task force went out to Iceland and drained all experienced officers and non-commissioned officers from the organization. (All the regular Army men). Before this time, the men had been given instruction in the erection and operation of the SCR-270-B, under careful supervision. After the task force left, personnel took over the entire work themselves and learned by doing and experimenting, since there were no trained personnel to instruct them." [235]

505th Signal Operations Company Aircraft Warning

"During the time that the First and Second Aircraft Warning Companies were in training, the 505th Signal Operating Company AW was activated at Maxwell Field, Alabama, late in June 1941.... The 505th Signal Operations Company AW joined the First and Second Warning Companies at Mitchel Field and groups from these three units along with members of the Signal Headquarters and Headquarters Company AW and the First Operations Company AW formed the Composite Aircraft Warning Company about the middle of August 1941 for the purpose of participating in the Louisiana Maneuvers. The Second Operations Company which had been activated at Mitchel Field at the same time as the Second Aircraft Warning Company had since (Spring of 1941) been assigned to the Third Interceptor Command and was stationed at Drew Field, Florida.

---

[235] *Ibid.*, pp. 2-4

Members of the 505th Signal Operations Company AW were trained in the operation of Information and Filter Centers through the use of wooden table maps and canned messages phoned to the plotters over EE 8A lines. This instruction went on until the assignment of the 505th personnel to Information and Filter Centers along the Eastern Seaboard on September 11, 1941."[236]

Louisiana Maneuvers

"Immediately after its formation, the Composite Aircraft Warning Company went on maneuvers in the vicinity of Natchitoches, Louisiana, during late August and the month of September. The 270-B units were shipped by train while the personnel and the 268 units traveled by motor convoy to the opening point."[237]

With maneuvers completed, the members of the First and Second Aircraft Warning Companies left Fort Benning, Georgia on October 1, 1941 and established detachments with their accompanying radar equipment at Accomac, Virginia, Bethany Beach, Delaware, and Longport, New Jersey to participate in the Northeastern Seaboard AW problem which was carried on from October 9th to 16th.

Northeastern Seaboard Problem

"505th personal were sent to Information Centers (ICs) and Fighter Control Centers (FCs) along the east coast in September 1941 to prepare for the October maneuvers.[238] The First and Second Aircraft Warning Companies established detachments and radar equipment for east coast during the northeast maneuvers October 9-16 1941.

For the maneuvers, four groups of FCs and ICs, and aircraft warning and operations detachments were established with headquarters at Boston, New York, Philadelphia, and Norfolk.

After the northeast maneuvers, skeleton crews were left at the FCs and ICs while the remaining personnel returned to Mitchel Field, and the detachments at radar sites returned to Fort Dix about the first of December 1941."[239]

---

[236] Ibid., pp. 4-5
[237] Ibid., p. 5
[238] Ibid., p. 5
[239] Ibid., p. 8

Norfolk Fighter Wing

The first appearance of military personnel at Norfolk came in August or September 1941 to lay the groundwork to install an FC. An office was set up in the Chesapeake and Potomac Telephone Company Building, and the Post Office building was used for volunteer training.[240]
They quartered, in makeshift fashion, in the City Armory, Norfolk, Virginia. [241]

From 9 to 16 October 1941, for the First Air Force test exercise of the air defenses of the Eastern Coast, the First Provisional Aircraft Warning Company was directed to occupy Derax [radar][242] sites at Bethany Beach, DL, Cape Henry, VA and Kitty Hawk, NC with Headquarters at Norfolk, Virginia for the purpose of providing instrumental warning service in the operation of Information and Filter Centers as directed by the Signal Officer, First Interceptor Command.[243]

After the field exercises most of the military personnel and only a nucleus of Signal Corps personal remained at Fort Story, N.C near Norfolk.

Eastern Aircraft Warning Service

With the outbreak of war on 8 December 1941, the skeleton crews at the Filter Centers and Information Centers worked 12-15 hour shifts until assistance arrived in late January.[244] Also, on December 8th a convoy of several reporting units departed from Fort Dix, New Jersey for various locations along the East Coast. Two of these units were dispatched to cover the areas south of the entrance to Chesapeake Bay. One unit operated at Virginia Beach, VA and the other at Kitty Hawk, NC. Both units formed the 659th Signal AW Reporting Company, Frontier that was activated on January 15, 1942.[245]

---

[240] Unit History of the Norfolk Fighter Wing, Part I, up to 31 December 42, U.S. Air Force History Museum
[241] Ibid., p. 1
[242] Derax for an early name for radar.
[243] Unit History of the 609th Signal AW Company, Regional, Period 15 September 1942 (Date of Activation) to 31 December 1942, U.S. Air Force History p. 1
[244] Ibid., p. 8
[245] Ibid., p. 2

On December 15, 1941, the First and Second Aircraft Warning Companies, and the 505th Signal Operations Company (AW) were deactivated, and formed into the 551st Signal Aircraft Warning Battalion, 501st and 502nd Aircraft Warning Regiments, and the 601st Signal Aircraft Plotting Company. On this date, unassigned Air Corps men at Fort Dix, New Jersey, unassigned men just having completed basic training at Fort Riley, Kansas, Fort Bragg, North Carolina, and Camp Croft, South Carolina were assigned to these units.[246]

Originally, these units were intended to be tactical, but due to the large number of untrained men coming in so suddenly, they were organized into training units on January 17, 1942, and a schedule of training classes was established.[247]

On January 15, 1941, the First Fighter Command activated the 609th Signal Plotting Company and the 659th Signal Reporting Company Frontier were attached to the Norfolk Air Defense Region and composed of personnel stationed at Norfolk, Fort Story, and Kitty Hawk. These units were later deactivated on September 14, 1942, and integrated into the 609th Sig Aircraft Warning Company, Regional that was activated on September 15, 1942. Similar units were established at the Boston, New York, and Philadelphia Fighter Wings.[248]

The Norfolk Air Defense Wing was activated on August 11, 1942, and the 609th Plotting Company and the 659th Reporting Company were attached to the new wing.[249] "The command was responsible for the following:
Conduct of the active air defense.
All activities within the Information Center.
The tactical employment of Derax [radar] equipment.
The tactical employment of pursuit force.
Operational controls of Antiaircraft Units .....
Coordination of liaison personnel ....."[250]

Enemy capabilities in the Norfolk area were submarines and surface raiders, and aircraft from surface raiders. Also, Germany had one completed aircraft carrier and

---

[246] Unit Histories of the 551st Battalion and 501st Regiment
[247] Memorandum for: AFCC Files, Subject: Conference on Training Program for Production of AWS personnel, January 17, 1942, Air Defense Section, Headquarters Air Force Combat Command, Bolling Field, D.C.
[248] Unit Histories of the 601st, 607th, 608th, and 609th Signal Aircraft Warning Companies, Frontier.
[249] Ibid., p. 7
[250] Ibid., p. 18

there were supposed to be four large converted merchant ships equipped to catapult four heavy bombers and three more were supposed to be nearing completion.[251]

The Wilmington Air Defense Region came under tactical and administrative control of the Norfolk Air Defense Wing on August 12, 1942. The 603rd Signal Air Warning Plotting Company and the 660th Signal Aircraft Warning Reporting Company, Frontier were attached to the Wilmington Air Defense Region, and they were integrated to form the 603rd Signal Aircraft Warning Company, Regional [252] in the fall of 1942.

The 4th WAAC Operations Company AWS and the 27th WAAC Filter Company AWS were activated and attached to Norfolk Air Wing on September 30, 1942.[253]

609th Signal AW Company, Regional

On 15 September 1942 both the 659th Signal AW Reporting Company, Frontier and the 609th plotting Company were consolidated and the 609th Signal AW Company Regional was born.[254]

"The 609th Signal Aircraft Warning Company was assigned as an integral part of the Norfolk Fighter Wing at Norfolk, Virginia. The mission of the fighter wing was to direct defense against hostile air operations, and to protect a definite area from attack by enemy aircraft."[255]

"The Company Headquarters detachment in Norfolk was organized with an Adjutant, a Personnel Officer, a Training Officer, a Supply Officer, and a Transportation Officer, all of whom served as staff to the Company Commander."[256]

All functions of the Signal Company came under the supervision of a Wing Signal Officer…. Who was responsible directly to" the Wing Commander.[257] "The mission of the organization was to give early warning of the approach of enemy aircraft

---

[251] Ibid., pp. 18-19
[252] Ibid., p. 8
[253] Ibid., p. 9
[254] Ibid., p. 2
[255] Unit History of the 609th Signal AW Company, Regional, Period 1 January 1943 to 30 June 1944 (Date of Disbandment), U.S. Air Force History p. 1
[256] Ibid., p. 27
[257] Ibid., p. 1

through the deployment of Radar Units strategically placed along the Eastern Coastline."[258]

"With the uncertainty which existed through the country early in 1942 with respect to hostile attack, attention originally was focused exclusively on operations.[259] However, in the latter part of 1942, as conditions became more settled, attention was directed towards the training of personnel."[260]

" The company was given the… mission of training personnel and was required to furnish cadres for overseas duty and for newly activated units. "One of the chief problems which the Signal Company had confronting it during its entire existence was the problem of effecting a happy wedlock between the operational function with which it was charged and the training mission which was imposed on it and given greater emphasis as time went on."[261]

"This imposed a heavy burden upon the organization. The training program interfered with operations, and the requirement to furnish cadres reduced efficiency through loss of key personnel."[262] The objective of the training was twofold:

Training in military occupational specialty to fill positions going to overseas. Training of new soldiers – Basic training and continuous refresher training to maintain the efficiency and discipline of a military organization[263]

Company Headquarters had been located in the basement of the U.S. Post Office Building On Granby Street.[264] EM of Headquarters Detachment at Norfolk were housed on two floors of the Monticello Hotel in downtown Norfolk.[265] "

"The company was divided into five components…..: First Reporting Detachment, Virginia Beach, Virginia, Second Reporting Detachment, Kitty Hawk, North Carolina,

---

[258] Ibid., p. 3
[259] Ibid., p. 4
[260] Ibid., p. 5
[261] Ibid., p. 14
[262] Ibid., p. 5
[263] Ibid., pp. 14-15
[264] Ibid., p. 36
[265] Ibid., p. 35

Filter Center, Richmond, Virginia, Filter Center, Roanoke, Virginia, and Information Center and Headquarters, Norfolk, Virginia."[266]

"The two reporting detachments were charged with the operation of Radar units and with the transmission of reports to the Information Center at Norfolk, and each reporting detachment consisted of two reporting platoons. One of the platoons manned a SCR 270D Radar unit for distant seaward search and the other manned a SCR 516 unit for close-in search and tracking missions.[267] Both Virginia Beach and Kitty Hawk had four trained dogs used to patrol with sentinels at night.[268]

"Kitty Hawk and Fort Story were both under strength in 1942, due chiefly to the drain on personnel for cadres by Mitchell Field. About 60% of the personnel were at that time untrained and the units were 65% under Table of Organization strength."[269] The allotment of enlisted men for the 609th Signal Company AW Regional was 327 enlisted men.[270] On December 1, 1942, the 609th Signal Company AW Regional, Second Detachment (Platoons C & D) had 64 personnel, 6 officers and 58 enlisted men 60% understrength to T/O.[271]

For the First Reporting Detachment the SCR 516 was located at 115th Street and the SCR 270 was located at 120th Street in Virginia Beach, VA. In February 1943 personnel of the First Detachment moved from Fort Story to the radar site at 115th Street, Virginia Beach.[272]

"Early in 1943, the radar reporting unit at Kitty Hawk was divided into two platoons of about forty-five men each. Each platoon had a separate Commanding Officer. In the later part of January 1943, a Detachment Commander was appointed and both platoons operated as one detachment.[273] As of December 1, 1942, the 609th Signal Company AW Regional, Second Detachment (Platoons C & D) had a permanent SRC 270C with a SRC 516 unit being installed about a quarter of a mile southeast of the 270-C which will be in operation about December 10, 1942.[274]

---

[266] Ibid., p. 3
[267] Ibid., p. 3
[268] Ibid., pp. 9-10
[269] Ibid., p. 11
[270] Ibid., Appendix II(a), Allotment of Grades – AWS Units, E.D.C.
[271] Ibid., Appendix VI, Report of Technical Inspection of Radar Stations of the Norfolk Air Defense Wing, p. 6
[272] Ibid., p. 37
[273] Ibid., p. 39
[274] Ibid., Appendix VI, p. 9

At Kitty Hawk "The men constructed several of their own buildings and built a plank road across the sand. There were plumbing facilities. A well point was made and later three other were dug. The men were transported [to Manteo] and to a nearby dance pavilion weekly. They were also transported to churches each Sunday."[275]

"For a time, a platoon of infantry was stationed across the road only a few hundred yards from the site. The primary mission of the infantry was protection of the radar site. Late in 1943, however the infantry was withdrawn."[276]

The 609th Aircraft Warning Company, Regional was deactivated in June 1944.[277]

Inactivation

With the war turning in Pacific, North Africa, and Italy in early 1943, decisions announced in September 1943 began the dismantling of the continental air defense network. "On 20 September 1943 the War Department put all observation posts and filter centers on alert status."[278]

"In November 1943 radar stations on the Pacific coast and those along the Atlantic south of Kitty Hawk ceased to operate on a 24-hour-per –day schedule."[279]

The Joint Chiefs made a decision to inactivate the AWS net in April 1944.[280]

"During June and July [1944] the radar net was curtailed, the fighter wings and regions were disbanded, and the remaining filter and information centers were closed."[281]

---

[275] Ibid., pp. 40-41
[276] Ibid., p. 10
[277] Unit History of the 609st Signal Aircraft Warning Company, Regional period 1 January 1943 to 30 June 1944 (Date of disbandment)
[278] The Army Air Forces in World War II, Men, Men and Planes, Volume VI, Edited by W. F. Craven and J. L. Cate, University of Chicago Press, Chicago, Illinois, 1955. p. 114.
[279] Ibid., p.114
[280] Ibid., p. 115
[281] Ibid., p. 115

BIBLIOGRAPHY

57th Fighter Group, Photographs by James C. "Wabbit" Hare, www.57thfightergroup.org

65th Fighter Squadron, Morning Report, August 21, 1945

65th Fighter Squadron, Morning Report, October 23, 1945

65th Fighter Squadron Morning Report, August 5, 1945, Passenger list for the Sea Owl

65th Fighter Squadron Morning Report, July 22, 1945

65th Fighter Squadron Morning Report, July 22, 1945

65th Fighter Squadron, Morning Report, August 21, 1945

65th Fighter Squadron, Morning Report, August 6, 1945

65th Fighter Squadron, War Diary, August 1945

65th Fighter Squadron, War Diary, July 1945

65th Fighter Squadron, War Diary, June 1945

65th Fighter Squadron Morning Report, July 22, 1945, and 65th Fighter Squadron Morning Report, August 5, 1945, Passenger list of the Sea Owl, Enclosure #1 to M/R 28 Jun 45

66th Fighter Squadron, War Diary, August 1945

78th Fighter Control Squadron, War Diary, November 1944

551st Signal Aircraft Warning Battalion, Historical Report 1, October 1943 to December 1943

594th Co A War Diary, June 1944

594th Co A, War Diary, May, 1944

594th History, The War & the 594th

594th War Diary Co A; November, 1944

594th War Diary Co A, September 1944

594th War Diary, Headquarters and Plotting Co, June 1945

594th War Diary, June 1945

594th, Rpt Co A Morning Reports, June 13, 1945

594th, Rpt Co A Morning Reports, June 17, 1945

609th Morning Report, November 1942

609th Morning Report, Platoon D, November 1942

Annual Report of Medical Department, Keystone Radio Schools Company, Hollidaysburg, PA, January 4, 1943

Camp Grant (Illinois), Wikipedia

Camp Grant Area Map (Rockford, Illinois) Illinois Digital Archives Illinois State Library, http://www.idaillinois.org/cdm/ref/collection/rockfordo1/id/131

Camp Patrick Henry, https://en.wikipedia.org/wiki/Camp_Patrick_Henry

Declaration of Surplus Real Property, File No: CE 602(Radar Station #14. Kitty Hawk, N.C.) to Surplus Property Board, Washington 25, D.C.

Diary of the 594th Signal Aircraft Warning Battalion

Draft text at end of the Diary of the 594th Aircraft Warning Battalion

Enlisted Record and Report of Separation and Honorable Discharge, Stanley J. Grant, 10 October 1945

French Cruiser Emile Bertin, https://en.wikipedia.org/wiki/French_cruiser_%C3%89mile_Bertin

Camp Grant, https://en.wikipedia.org/wiki/Camp_Grant_(illinois)

SCR-270, https://en.wikipedia.org/wiki/SCR-270

SCR-527, https://en.wikipedia.org/wiki/SCR-527

Signal Corps Laboratories, https://en.wikipedia.org/wiki/Signal_Corps_Laboratories

Camp Miles Standish, https:/en.wikipedia.org/Camp_Miles_Standish

Keystone Radio Schools Graduation Ceremony Program, Photographs 096D, 096E, 096F

Kitty Hawk Quadrangle, N3600-W753015, Dare County, North Carolina, 1941-1942

Memo and attachment dated April 25, 1941, Headquarters GHQ Air Force, Bolling Field, D.C., Subject: Aircraft Warning Services and Air Defense, to: The Adjutant General, Washington, D.C., National Archives, Atlanta, GA

Memorandum for: AFFCC Files, Subject: Conference on Training Program for Production of AWS personnel, January 17, 1942, Air Defense Section, Headquarters Air Force Combat Command, Bolling Field, D.C.

Morning Report, 594th Signal Aircraft Warning Battalion, December 11, 1943

Morning Report, 594th Signal Aircraft Warning Battalion, December 17, 1943

Morning Report, 609th Signal Aircraft Warning Company, Regional, November 1942

Morning Report, 609th Signal Aircraft Warning Company, Regional, December 1942

Morning Report, 609th Signal Aircraft Warning Company, Regional, January 1943

Morning Report, 609th Signal Aircraft Warning Company, Regional, March 1943

Morning Report, 659th Signal Aircraft Warning Company, Frontier, February 1942

Morning Report, 659th Signal Aircraft Warning Company, Frontier, May 1942

Morning Report, 659th Signal Aircraft Warning Company, Frontier, June 1942

Morning Report, 659th Signal Aircraft Warning Company, Frontier, September 1942

Official Photograph from U.S. Army Signal Corps, Hampton Roads Port of Embarkation in Newport News (1944) from Ahoy!, October-November-December 2015, The Mariner' Museum, 100 Museum Drive, Newport News, VA

Recorded interviews for grade school projects by Stanley Grant's granddaughter, Jennifer Grant, and his Grandson, Michael Johnson

Records Pertaining to Aircraft Warning Stations 1920-1941 from RG 111, National Archives Identifier: 6782669, Container Identifier: Box 3, HMS Entry Number(s): PI-155 52, National Archives, College Park, Maryland.

SCR-270, Wikipedia, https://en.wikipedia.org/wiki/SCR-270

Signal Corps Laboratories, Wikipedia, https://en.wikipedia.org/wiki/Signal_Corps_Laboratories

Special Order Number 5, 594th Signal Aircraft Warning Battalion, November 18, 1942

Stanley Grant and Helen Michalak Wedding License

T/5 Stanley Grant Keystone Radio Schools Diploma

The Army Air Forces in World War II, Men, Men and Planes, Volume VI, Chapter, Edited by W. F. Craven and J. L. Cate, University of Chicago Press, Chicago, Illinois, 1955

The SCR-527 and Photograph, https://en.wikipedia.org/wiki/SCR-527

Unit History of the 501st Regiment for Period December 1941 to December 1943

Unit History of the 609th Sig Aircraft Warning Company, Regional, Period January 1, 1943, to June 30, 1944 (Date of disbandment)

Unit History of the 609th Sig AW Company, Regional, Period September 15, 1942 to December 31, 1942 Appendix VI, Inspection Report, 2nd Reporting Detachment, Kitty Hawk, North Carolina, December 1, 1942

Unit History of the 609th Signal Aircraft Warning Company, Regional, Period September 15, 1942 to December 31, 1942

Unit History of the Norfolk Fighter Wing, Part I, up to 31 December 42

USS Cornelius Harnett, http://www.armed-guard.com/liberty.html

U.S.S. Corsica, *L'ile portes avions*, Dominique Taddei, Albiana, 2003.

West Jersey History Project, Historic Images of Burlington County NJ, Images of Burlington County NJ – Camp Dix/Fort Dix
http://westjerseyhistory.org/images/Burlington/wrightstown-dix/index.shtml

www.ingramcontent.com/pod-product-compliance
Lightning Source LLC
Chambersburg PA
CBHW081917130526
44581CB00019B/108